Poetry and Civilization

Photograph by B. Anthony Stewart. Courtesy National Geographic Society.

Poetry and Civilization

Essays by GEORGE FRISBIE WHICHER

Collected and Edited by

HARRIET FOX WHICHER

NEW YORK / RUSSELL & RUSSELL

To Amherst College

"May her sons in her, and she
through them, keep faith in human brotherhood, yet never
fail of devotion to strenuous liberty of mind and spirit."

GEORGE FRISBIE WHICHER, *New Year's Day*, 1939

Preface

Tʜɪs volume of essays and speeches, which is published after George Whicher's death, represents a small selection from the mass of material he left in his files. It was fortunate that he had no major work in progress, for his trenchant writing could bear little addition or subtraction from another hand. Nor was there much unpublished work; he was constantly writing, on demand, to fulfill literary or academic obligations. My desire in editing these papers has been simply to bring into more permanent form a few of the articles now scattered in the bound volumes of magazines. I have made slight changes in the text—mostly omissions—only when the lapse of time has blunted the point of certain references.

None of the many reviews published in the *Herald-Tribune Book Review* between 1924 and 1954 have been reprinted here. They served their purpose at the time of writing, often with telling effect, but could hardly be separated from their context. Yet circumstances of time and place cling close, in the memory of those who knew George Whicher, to everything here printed. To read his words is to feel with Robert Frost that the hours of daylight gather atmosphere. "Poetry and Civilization" was a speech given at a dinner in Honolulu at the end of a halcyon spring in Hawaii, where he had been visiting professor at the university. The table was set outdoors, among the hibiscus and oleander bushes, and yellow plumeria blossoms strewed the white tablecloth; the speaker's head emerged from a *lei* of red carnations. "Out for Stars" is intimately connected with a summer in Ripton, Vermont, which he spent as Robert Frost's close neighbor. Yet it recalls winters as well, conversations before the fire in our study in Amherst or under the falling snow on the road to Pelham, incomparable talk between two friends over a period of forty years. Echoes of their discussions of poetry may be found in "Unit and Universe . . . ," which reflects on the meaning of Emerson's "Uriel" for Robert Frost. The paper on "The Future of the American Novel" also intertwines threads of time and place. It was given as a speech at a writers' conference at Grinnell College, where George Whicher's father and mother had spent their undergraduate years and graduated in 1882.

No volume of George Whicher's work would be complete without a word on Emily Dickinson, whose poetry was his chief interest and preoccupation after 1935, when he began writing *This Was a Poet*. In January 1947 he was asked to give the Percy Turnbull Memorial Lectures at the Johns Hopkins University. "For the purpose of commemorating the name of their son, who died in 1887, Mr. and Mrs. Lawrence Turnbull of Baltimore made provision [in 1889] for lectures on poetry to be given before the University by some scholar who has gained distinction as a writer or critical student of poetry." Professor Whicher chose to speak on Emily Dickinson. The lecture here printed is the third of the series of six delivered to a friendly and appreciative audience. The little narrative sketch, "Pursuit of the Overtakeless," carries its own atmosphere and needs no comment.

But it was to Amherst College that George Whicher dedicated his life. He loved it from the time he entered as a freshman in 1906 to the day of his death and gladly lived his life in the shadow of its old brick buildings on the hilltop overlooking the Connecticut Valley. He loved the association of men and books and the College's loyalty to its inheritance of freedom of the mind. He spoke often in the chapel—a simple and beautiful New England meetinghouse —and just two days before his death had given there one of his wise and witty seven-minute speeches, a brief commemoration of the centenary of the publication of Thoreau's *Walden.* Three of his longer speeches are reprinted here. The faculty speaker at the Senior Chapel exercises is always chosen by the seniors themselves and is usually elected a member of the class. George Whicher was immensely proud of the honor thus conferred upon him several times. In May 1954 he was elected a member of the senior class *in memoriam.*

The circumstances of George Whicher's life can be briefly summarized. He was born at Lawrenceville, New Jersey, on November 5, 1889, and spent most of his childhood in Brooklyn, where his father was professor of classics at Packer Institute. From the Brooklyn Polytechnic Preparatory School he went to Amherst College, from which he graduated *summa cum laude* in 1910. The three years after his graduation were spent in New York City, studying for his Ph.D. degree at Columbia University. From 1913 to 1915 he taught at the University of Illinois under the aegis of Stuart P. Sherman, whom, as he himself said, he idolized, and whose influence upon his later work was profound. In 1915 he came to Amherst as associate professor of English, became full professor in 1922, and remained on the faculty until his sudden death on March 7, 1954. During several summers and leaves of absence he taught at the Bread Loaf School of English (Middlebury College, Vermont), and the universities of Michigan, Minnesota, and Hawaii. During the year 1952–1953 he was Fulbright Lecturer at the University of Istanbul.

He wrote constantly. In an obituary notice in the May 1954 number of *American Literature*, Professor James Woodress writes:

George Whicher's writing always reflected his meticulous scholarship and profound awareness of the American past. His study of Emily Dickinson, *This Was a Poet* (1938), remains the standard book on its subject—a model of narrative biography and perceptive interpretation—and his contribution to *The Literature of the American People* (1951) is an extraordinarily acute ordering of the chaos of twentieth-century literature. His *Walden Revisited* (1945), moreover, is an authoritative essay, dense in substance, free from pedantry, and illuminated by imaginative understanding. Besides being completely at home in American literature, he cared deeply for European and classical culture, as evidenced in his graceful translations from the Goliard poets and Horace.

One of his most popular books is *Mornings at 8:50: Brief Evocations of the Past for a College Audience*, a collection of his chapel speeches at Amherst College; these were biographies in miniature which attempted "to reveal the dimension of time to that most timeless of mortals, the American undergraduate." He edited the *Amherst Graduates' Quarterly* from 1919 to 1932, served on the editorial boards of *American Literature* and the *American Scholar*, brought out several anthologies, notably *Poetry of the New England Renaissance* (1950), and served as trustee of Marlboro College in Vermont and of the Jones Library in Amherst.

Pleasant interludes in his life were the result of his fondness for travel. Before his fiftieth year he took this pleasure often on foot, on the Appalachian Trail or over the stony roads of the Gaspé Peninsula. Occasional leaves of absence were spent in the south and west of the United States; in Paris and London, with excursions to Italy and Majorca; in Hawaii; in Turkey and the Near East. There were summers in Vermont, in Bermuda, in Nova Scotia. He played an excellent game of tennis. Another of his purest delights was the discreet collecting of rare books. George Whicher's library was well known to bibliophiles, for he was a distinguished collector of Americana. All these forms of recreation were welcome, for he lived his life intensely, as his nervous, sensitive writing attests. Love of family and friends, urbanity and gentleness of life, and freedom of thought were essential to him. The ugliness of bad thinking, of malice or passion or tyranny in any form, hurt and horrified him; from them he was protected only by his humorous understanding of human nature and his great charity. In times of strain his innate courtesy supported him like a fine kind of strength.

The making of this book would not have been possible without the help of Amherst College. The instant and generous response of the trustees to the suggestion of such a volume was gratifying in the extreme. One can only realize that they too loved George Whicher and wanted to honor his memory. In this last tribute, as in the close association of nearly fifty years, Amherst has been truly his Alma Mater. The book is dedicated to the College in the words of her New Year's greeting for 1939, written by George Whicher himself.

HARRIET FOX WHICHER

Amherst, Massachusetts
January 1955

Acknowledgments

I wish to express my gratitude to the editors of the *National Geographic Magazine* for their permission to use a black-and-white reproduction of the photograph printed in color in that magazine in March 1950. They have been generous with help as well as with permission. Of the photograph George Whicher once said that it showed him "examining a letter by Emily Dickinson while reclining on the bosom of Sabrina," and added, "What more can a college teacher desire?"

I wish to thank the following publications or publishing agencies for permission to reprint articles:

The *Amherst Graduates' Quarterly* for the Senior Chapel speech "The Soul of a College" (August 1930).
The *Atlantic Monthly* for "Out for Stars: A Meditation on Robert Frost" (May 1943).
The Department of Public Instruction of the Territory of

Acknowledgments

Hawaii for "Poetry and Civilization," printed in the *Hawaii Educational Review* (December 1948).

Events Publishing Company, Inc., for "Unit and Universe . . . ," printed in *Forum* (July 1946).

The *Nation* for "Pursuit of the Overtakeless" (July 2, 1949).

I wish to thank the following publishers for permission to make quotations:

The Atlantic Monthly Press for a passage from *The Letters of William James* (1920), edited by his son, Henry James.

Jonathan Cape Limited for foreign rights for Robert Frost's poems listed below under Henry Holt and Company.

The Cornell University Press for a passage from *A Study of Literature: For Readers and Critics* (1948), by David Daiches.

Harper & Brothers for "That odd old man is dead a year" from *Bolts of Melody: New Poems of Emily Dickinson* (1945), edited by Mabel Loomis Todd and Millicent Todd Bingham. Copyright, 1945, by Millicent Todd Bingham.

Henry Holt and Company for "One Step Backward Taken"; for quotations from "Two Tramps in Mud Time," "Come In," and "Choose Something Like a Star"; and for fragmentary quotations from various other poems from *Complete Poems of Robert Frost*. Copyright, 1930, 1947, 1949, by Henry Holt and Company, Inc. Copyright, 1936, 1942, by Robert Frost. Reprinted by permission of the publishers.

For a fragmentary quotation from "Chicago" in *Chicago Poems* by Carl Sandburg. Copyright, 1916, by Henry Holt and Company, Inc. Copyright, 1944, by Carl Sandburg. Reprinted by permission of the publishers.

For a fragmentary quotation from *Collected Poems* by A. E. Housman. Copyright, 1940, by Henry Holt and Company, Inc. Reprinted by permission of the publishers.

Houghton Mifflin Company for a passage from *The Education*

Acknowledgments

of Henry Adams: An Autobiography (1918). Copyright, 1918, by the Massachusetts Historical Society.

For a fragmentary quotation from "Ars Poetica" in *Collected Poems, 1917–1952* (1952), by Archibald MacLeish.

Alfred A. Knopf, Inc., for a passage from *Lady Chatterley's Lover* (1928), by D. H. Lawrence.

Little, Brown & Company for "I tend my flowers for thee" and "The popular Heart is a cannon first" from *Poems of Emily Dickinson* (1937), copyright, 1929, by Martha Dickinson Bianchi; also for fragmentary quotations from various other poems, copyright, 1914 and 1929, by Martha Dickinson Bianchi.

The Macmillan Company for "Karma" from *Collected Poems of Edwin Arlington Robinson* (1937). Copyright, 1935 and 1937, by the Macmillan Company. Copyright, 1925, by E. A. Robinson.

For a passage from *Dostoievsky* (1947), by Janko Lavrin.

Random House for a quotation from "Under Which Lyre: A Reactionary Tract for the Times" in *Nones* (1951), by W. H. Auden.

The Society of Authors, as the Literary Representative of the Trustees of the Estate of the late A. E. Housman, and Messrs. Jonathan Cape, Ltd., publishers of A. E. Housman's *Collected Poems*, for foreign rights for a fragmentary quotation from A. E. Housman.

Professor Whicher would also have wished, I think, to acknowledge his indebtedness to W. S. Tyler's *History of Amherst College* and to Edward Hitchcock's *Reminiscences of Amherst College*.

Without the help, advice, and encouragement of my son, Stephen Whicher, I should never have undertaken even this small task of editing; with him it has been a happy venture.

HARRIET FOX WHICHER

Contents

Poetry and Civilization[1]

W HEN the first colonists left
Europe to come to the American wilderness, they left civilization behind them. Only a small part of its traditional
agencies for enriching life could be recreated in the New
World. Religion and education were valued so highly, in
New England at least, that they were immediately provided
for. Literature had to be largely sacrificed. The *Bay Psalm
Book* was a poor bit of salvage after the glories of Elizabethan poetry and drama. Michael Wigglesworth's *The Day
of Doom* was a bare substitute for the majesty of *Paradise
Lost*. Architecture, painting, and sculpture could not be enjoyed for a period of two hundred years, during which the

[1] An address given at the Annual Phi Kappa Phi Banquet held in
Honolulu in May 1947. Professor Whicher was visiting professor
of English at the University of Hawaii from February to August
1947.

1

need to settle a new country ever expanding westward, and later to forward its industrial development, assumed paramount importance. As a result Americans as a people lost their sense of the ministry of the arts to the human spirit.

In the course of the nineteenth century many efforts were made to supply the deficiency. From the time of the Hartford Wits to that of the Transcendentalists the desire to produce an original American literature was an acknowledged aim of young writers. Pilgrims to Europe brought home objects of virtu for the adornment of their houses, taste in public buildings gradually improved, and large numbers of paintings were acquired and exhibited in museum galleries. But all this effort did relatively little to restore art to a functional place in society. Science usurped its sphere. Even yet the plain man in the street has little conception of what the arts are good for, nor has he learned the rudiments of how to establish relations with a painting or poem. A realistic museum curator recently held a stop watch on the visitors. Not one was observed to spend more than sixty seconds before any one painting in the gallery, and the average time was just under ten seconds. Certainly this indicates an excessive reliance on the adage that he who runs may read.

In contrast let us remind ourselves of the pains that a true connoisseur is willing to take to assure himself of the quality of a work of art. For the honor of our nation he shall be an American. Henry Adams, on returning to Washington in 1892, went at once to the cemetery at Rock Creek to see the bronze figure which St. Gaudens had designed to mark the spot where Mrs. Adams was buried. He speaks first of his own prolonged and searching study of the sculptor's work.

Naturally every detail interested him; every line; every touch of the artist; every change of light and shade; every point of relation; every possible doubt of St. Gaudens's correctness of taste or feeling; so that, as the spring approached, he was apt to stop there often to see what the figure had to tell him that was new; but, in all that it had to say, he never once thought of questioning what it meant. He supposed its meaning to be the one commonplace about it—the oldest idea known to human thought. He knew that if he asked an Asiatic its meaning, not a man, woman, or child from Cairo to Kamtchatka would have needed more than a glance to reply. . . . The interest of the figure was not in its meaning, but in the response of the observer.

This is the attitude of a man highly sensitized to the values of art and patient in discovering them. But Adams then goes on to describe with withering irony the inability of the average American to respond to a work of art in appropriate terms.

As Adams sat there, numbers of people came, for the figure seemed to have become a tourist fashion, and all wanted to know its meaning. Most took it for a portrait-statue, and the remnant were vacant-minded in the absence of a personal guide. . . . The only exceptions were the clergy, who taught a lesson even deeper. One after another brought companions there, and, apparently fascinated by their own reflection, broke out passionately against the expression they felt in the figure of despair, of atheism, of denial. Like the others, the priest saw only what he brought. Like all great artists, St. Gaudens held up the mirror and no more. The American layman had lost sight of ideals; the American priest had lost sight of faith. Both were more American than the old, half-witted soldiers who denounced the wasting, on a mere grave, of money which should have been given for drink.

Poetry and Civilization

A similar helplessness of Americans when high and genuine artistry is encountered may be illustrated in the attitude toward literature of men who in other respects are unusually gifted and well informed. The following passage from a letter of William James to his brother Henry in 1907 is exceptionally revealing. The Harvard philosopher was writing to acknowledge his appreciation of a recent book in the novelist's famous "later manner," a book which he could hardly help conceding was "in its peculiar way *supremely great.*" But he then added:

You know how opposed your whole "third manner" of execution is to the literary ideals which animate my crude and Orson-like breast, mine being to say a thing in one sentence as straight and explicit as it can be made, and then to drop it forever; yours being to avoid naming it straight, but by dint of breathing and sighing all round and round it, to arouse in the reader who may have had a similar perception already (Heaven help him if he hasn't!) the illusion of a solid object . . . wholly out of impalpable materials, air, and the prismatic interferences of light, ingeniously focused by mirrors upon empty space.

After this fraternal poke in the ribs, William proceeded to give Henry advice in good elder brother fashion:

And so I say now, give us *one* thing in your older directer manner, just to show that, in spite of your paradoxical success in this unheard of method, you *can* still write according to accepted canons. . . . For gleams and innuendoes and felicitous verbal insinuations you are unapproachable, but the *core* of literature is solid. Give it to us *once* again! The bare perfume of things will not support existence, and the effect of solidity you reach is but perfume and simulacrum.

4

Poetry and Civilization

What Henry James had reached, after a lifetime of arduous trial and error, was a method of writing fiction which enabled him to attain intensities approximating the intensity of poetry. Hence it was necessary for him to rely on indirection. After all the highest aim of literary art is not to say a thing straight in one sentence and then to drop it forever. "Poetry," declared Edwin Arlington Robinson, "is a language that tells us, through a more or less emotional reaction, something that cannot be said." And George Santayana amplified the same idea when he wrote: "But poetry is something secret and pure, some magical perfection lighting up the mind for a moment, like reflections in the water, playful and fugitive. Your true poet catches the charm of something or anything, dropping the thing itself." Because Henry James and other writers and critics after him have thought long and hard about the nature of literary art, we understand its capacities and methods somewhat better today than even an intellectually keen man like William James could in the first decades of the century. We are recovering the sense of poetry's place in the scheme of civilized living which has been lost sight of since the seventeenth century.

We know that since the poet's business is to deal with highly complex human situations in their totality, he cannot confine himself to a language of literal statement, nor can what he has to say be reduced to an abstract formula of meaning apart from the poem itself. The poem's full meaning *is* the poem, a dynamic structure of tensions that can be felt but only partially described. The poet works by indirection and suggestion. His method will be analogical rather than logical, and he will proceed by a series of con-

Poetry and Civilization

tradictions and qualifications, or in terms that are now fashionable with critics, by paradox, ambiguity, and irony. The truth of a poetic symbol is not determined by absolutes external to the poem but by its vital relation to its context. It is in essence dramatic. And finally poetry is at its peak of achievement when it manages to contain and harmonize whole systems of conflicting values. One may almost say that poetry is the art of suggesting how differing values may be adjusted without sacrificing any of them to make the adjustment easy.

Poetry is, therefore, by no means an idle amusement nor a merely ornamental accomplishment. It is one of the basic ways of understanding experience, one of the mental instruments by means of which we can achieve a certain reconciliation with our destiny as men. In general we possess two modes of apprehending life, that of the analytic reason and that of the synthesizing imagination. The two are not necessarily opposed, but the intellectual history of the nineteenth century has been a tragic story of factitious oppositions between the two and of mistaken attempts to rely upon the analytic mode of science to the exclusion of the imaginative mode of poetry. In consequence the power to deal with life imaginatively, with a full realization of all its implications, has become almost a lost art in the West, so much so that Henry Adams was able to make his caustic reflections on the blindness of Americans to values that Orientals would have comprehended at a glance. As a verbal art poetry has suffered more than music or painting from the intrusions of incongruous attitudes. It has been interpreted in terms appropriate to scientific statement and judged as though its whole duty were to embody truisms in mnemonic rhyme. Hence it has been frequently denatured and robbed of significance.

Poetry and Civilization

Our age, intoxicated by the operational control over the physical world made possible by the marvelous advances of science, has forgotten to its acute disadvantage the equal need of cultivating an imaginative grasp of human attitudes and response through the arts. Ironically enough, at the very moment when almost unlimited power over the physical world is within man's reach, he finds himself unable to enjoy the full fruits of material control because of the hopeless deterioration of his relations with other men. When maturity of mind is lacking, the crude adolescent urge to dominate the world stands ready waiting to fill the void.

In an article on the tragic sense of Eugene O'Neill, Professor Joseph Wood Krutch of Columbia suggests that the probable reason why O'Neill's plays have been received with a striking mixture of approval and disapproval is that, unlike Ibsen, O'Neill's approach to his material has been essentially poetic. Most modern playwrights, on the other hand, have written sociological drama which assumes that our predicaments are remediable. "They are, to put it somewhat differently, concerned with problems properly so called, while O'Neill, like most great tragic dramatists, is concerned with dilemmas." If this is a tenable idea, it would go to show that a large number of Americans are unable to recognize poetry when they encounter it or to understand its objects. They have forgotten that underneath the tameness and rationality of modern life lie the same dark questions of fate that troubled Aeschylus.

To become wise, that is to become reconciled to fate, through the arts is not an easy matter. It demands patience and a habit of contemplation, as illustrated in the long study that Adams made of the shrouded figure imagined by St. Gaudens to symbolize the eternal mystery. A sonnet that

7

epitomizes in a single incident an era in our history and a permanent trait of human nature is not to be lightly absorbed and discarded as one treats the daily paper. It demands long pondering to perceive all the rays that are concentrated to make the single point of radiance, and the long pondering is what enriches life and differentiates us from the brutes.

Let me give one illustration by comparing a respectable historical work, a matter of plain statement merely, with a literary creation not too complicated to be read aloud. In 1904 Miss Ida M. Tarbell published her pioneer investigation of an American trust—*The History of the Standard Oil Company*, a factual and impartial work which set forth among other things the ruthless methods employed by a successful corporation to crush its rivals and to secure a virtual monopoly of a vital commodity. Miss Tarbell's book caused something of a sensation in its time, but it now gathers dust on the shelves. The situations and practices that it describes are largely outdated or outlawed, and the work retains only, as we say, a historical interest. But I suspect that the essence of Miss Tarbell's demonstration, the germ of perception that gave it vitality, is preserved very nearly intact in the following sonnet by E. A. Robinson. Perhaps it is not unfair to recall in advance the first John D. Rockefeller's habit of handing out a bright new dime whenever he felt it appropriate to give a gratuity.

> Christmas was in the air and all was well
> With him, but for a few confusing flaws
> In divers of God's images. Because
> A friend of his would neither buy nor sell,
> Was he to answer for the axe that fell?
> He pondered; and the reason for it was,

8

Partly, a slowly freezing Santa Claus
Upon the corner, with his beard and bell.

Acknowledging an improvident surprise,
He magnified a fancy that he wished
The friend whom he had wrecked were here again.
Not sure of that, he found a compromise;
And from the fulness of his heart he fished
A dime for Jesus who had died for men.

It will take some time for the reader of this sonnet to exhaust its ironic implications, and long after the Standard Oil Company is out of mind like its predecessor the whaling industry, the poem will remain as fresh and pertinent as it is today, since its subject is an aspect of the perpetual struggle within the heart of man. Possibly a patient scrutiny of the poem will make it less easy for one to practice without discomfort the kind of self-delusion that Robinson has scathingly exposed. A minor consequence might lie in the embarrassment of giving less than a quarter henceforth when the collection plate comes round.

If our civilization is not to become a breeding ground of cruel and soulless animals, the capacities of mind and heart that poetry is peculiarly organized to foster will need to be deliberately cultivated. Otherwise, as Hamlet long ago remarked and as we have had bitter occasion to observe in recent years, "things rank and gross in nature" will possess our unweeded garden.

There are two fields of activity where imaginative insight and wisdom are especially demanded, in economic and social adjustments and in education. These are fields where we are under especial temptation to assume that analysis and rational adjustment are the only instrumentalities re-

9

quired, though in both fields nonrational factors play an uncertain part. I am not proposing to substitute poetic attitudes for the conclusions reached by scientific analysis. We need to learn all that economics and social anthropology and psychology can teach us. But scientific analysis of human problems that are involved with genuine dilemmas is not enough by itself. It invariably makes simplifications to facilitate the process of reaching a solution, and in doing so loses sight of essential values. The abstraction known as "economic man" is not all of human nature, but when economic thinking is translated into social action the distinction is sometimes forgotten. Then we find that even the best-intentioned social planning only imperfectly meets the requirements of actual situations. A more imaginative habit of mind might have saved us from blunders. We should have had a consultant in poetry on the staff.

An illustration may help to make clear what I mean. In dealing with the problem of unemployment, the social economist has as his paramount consideration the necessity of human livelihood. Each job available is a means to support the existence of one social unit. Sixty million workers, sixty million jobs—as simple as that, regardless of whether there are sixty million things worth doing. The important thing is that wealth should be distributed. Hence jobs are regarded as capillaries through which the life-giving fluid may reach the individual cells. Or something to that effect.

But now and then human beings cling in a disconcerting way to the elements that the economist discards as nonessential. A distinguished missionary mentioned the other day an incident in point that came to his attention in Micronesia. During the American occupation of the area, the inhabitants of a certain island were bidden to produce copra. They labored at the task with might and main, and by the time that the ship which was to collect their produce called they had one hundred tons on hand. It happened, however, that the ship was already partly loaded and had room for only thirty tons more. The responsible Navy administrator did all that was necessary to satisfy the economic man. He accepted the entire one hundred tons at the contract price, paid the natives for their work, took on board thirty tons, and dumped the surplus in the sea. Then to his surprise he found that he had a near rebellion on his hands. The islanders objected that they had put their energy, their time, their interest into the making of that copra, and they felt entitled to suppose that they were expending themselves for something that would be put to use. They were outraged that their product was not properly respected.

A poetic approach to the problem of unemployment would not attempt to simplify and solve a limited problem, but to contemplate, bring to light, and understand as many aspects of the situation as possible. A poet would try to see the matter from all angles and to test it in relation to all possible considerations. He would not be satisfied, in short, until he had as far as possible exhausted its human meaning. The subject of unemployment has in fact been handled by Robert Frost in his poem entitled "Two Tramps in Mud Time," which states a philosophy of labor from the point of view of a man who has worked much with his hands. The speaker in the poem is thoroughly enjoying the routine business of splitting wood and being outdoors on a day when spring makes its first hesitating appearance. At the moment two hulking tramps come in sight.

Poetry and Civilization

Out of the mud two strangers came
And caught me splitting wood in the yard.
And one of them put me off my aim
By hailing cheerily "Hit them hard!"
I knew pretty well why he dropped behind
And let the other go on a way.
I knew pretty well what he had in mind:
He wanted to take my job for pay.

. . . . .

The time when I most loved my task
These two must make me love it more
By coming with what they came to ask.
You'd think I never had felt before
The weight of an axe-head poised aloft,
The grip on earth of outspread feet.
The life of muscles rocking soft
And smooth and moist in vernal heat.

. . . . .

Nothing on either side was said.
They knew they had but to stay their stay
And all their logic would fill my head:
As that I had no right to play
With what was another man's work for gain.
My right might be love but theirs was need,
And where the two exist in twain
Theirs was the better right—agreed.

But yield who will to their separation,
My object in living is to unite
My avocation and my vocation
As my two eyes make one in sight.
Only where love and need are one,
And the work is play for mortal stakes,
Is the deed ever really done
For Heaven and the future's sakes.

Poetry and Civilization

The poet has made some concessions to the average reader and has come closer to direct statement than usual. But what is stated, and even more what is implied between the lines, is an emotional and impalpable factor that can be felt but not directly analyzed. Beyond the doing of a job for pay is the doing of it for fun, the doing of it as a fulfillment of the doer's nature, the doing of it as a challenge to his skill or his powers of endurance, the doing of it because it needs to be done, the doing of it because the task is part of a larger enterprise to which one is dedicated, like homemaking. Such motives, if slighted by a view that levels all values to economic ones, have a way of taking their revenges. Sometimes they emerge as crucial in determining men's actions against what makes for self-interest. Sometimes they remain to trouble the mind of one who has yielded too hastily to economic pressures. These things are not lost in the inclusive view of a poet.

One phrase in Frost's concluding lines demands a moment's further consideration: "And the work is play for mortal stakes." "Work is play" sounds like a well-worn paradox, but the metaphor is suddenly changed and deepened when the words "for mortal stakes" are added. The implication seems to be that what we give our hearts to is always a gamble, not something that can be scientifically predicated. In poetry the commitment, though earnest, must not have an air of desperation. The poet takes uncalculated risks. He ventures many opinions. It is the essence of the poetic method even in its serious moments to venture them lightly, trying on and discarding ideas as though they were changes of garments. Poetry is the play of the mind or it is nothing. Hence it is very disconcerting to people who would gladly persuade us that ideas are weapons and must not be taken out of the arsenal unless we intend to use them with murderous intent.

Poetry, then, offers us a universally available training ground for the exercise of thought and imagination. It provides a constant stimulus to the faculties of choice and discrimination, taste and judgment. It sharpens the perception of what is unlike in cases nearly similar so that false values may be separated from genuine ones. It speculates on the springs of human action and penetrates by imaginative sympathy into some of the mysteries of man's nature. It sets up concepts of form and order. It holds before the mind a standard of performance. Without some such exercise as poetry supplies, men's wits grow fat and dense, and their vision of the possibilities of achievement is narrowed. Ideas are viewed with suspicion and criticism is identified with disloyalty. The whole theory of self-government then falls to the ground, since as Herbert Read has put it in *The Politics of the Unpolitical*, "A free people must be a highly critical people." Most of our disasters begin with corruption of words.

Because of its serviceability in bringing the mind to maturity, poetry would seem to be ideally adapted to the purposes of education, and under the name of the Humanities it has long been held as fundamental in the acquiring of a liberal culture. Recently, however, its pre-eminence has been challenged, not I think because there is any actual conflict between the instrumentalities whereby men live, but because the limitations of a crowded curriculum set up factitious oppositions between subjects competing for room to flourish in. The more aggressive social sciences have not hesitated to describe the Humanities as a ragbag of unfounded superstitions and old wives' tales, and to suggest that the one hope of civilization is to rely exclusively on scientific analysis for the solution of all its dilemmas. But there is no good reason why we should limit ourselves to a fraction of our potential capacities. The inclusive disciplines of poetry, the arts, philosophy, and religion offer correctives of the partial conclusions. The maintenance of civilization depends on the cultivation to the fullest extent of both the great instruments of civilized living, not on the supplanting of either by the other.

The tendency of thinking in our era has set strongly in the direction of analytical techniques. To run the world as it is now constituted will demand multitudes of trained scientific workers, engineers, technicians, and experts in social control. There can be no argument concerning the need to produce them. They must and will be forthcoming, and our colleges and universities will be geared to turn them out. What needs to be fostered intentionally, since circumstances do not immediately require it, is the side of education necessary in the long run to keep humanity on an even keel. The poet has work to do in the world not less important and exacting than the work of the engineer and the scientist, and somewhat less likely to be done well. That work is in part to clear away the confusion due to pseudo-scientific thinking. It is also the business of the poet to maintain a mental climate in which it is possible to live a humane life. For our superheated time that duty often takes the form of air-conditioning by the injection of cooling humor.

For a current example one may turn to the Phi Beta Kappa poem, "Under Which Lyre," read at Harvard in June 1946, by W. H. Auden. The poet has been quick to sense an overserious tone in American college life since the war. He therefore attacks the pompous official attitude of learned dignitaries, ending his poem with what he calls a "Hermetic Decalogue" calculated to deflate the academic ego and let the mind relax.

> Thou shalt not do as the dean pleases,
> Thou shalt not write any doctor's thesis
>   On education,
> Thou shalt not worship projects nor
> Shalt thou or thine bow down before
>   Administration.
>
> Thou shalt not answer questionnaires
> Or quizzes upon World Affairs,
>   Nor with compliance
> Take any test. Thou shalt not sit
> With statisticians nor commit
>   A social science.
>
> Thou shalt not be on friendly terms
> With guys in advertising firms,
>   Nor speak with such
> As read the Bible for its prose,
> Nor, above all, make love to those
>   Who wash too much.
>
> Thou shalt not live within thy means
> Nor on plain water and raw greens.
>   If thou must choose
> Between the chances, choose the odd;
> Read the *New Yorker*; trust in God;
>   And take short views.

It is part of a proper education to know scientific tech-niques and also to be able to recognize the occasions when they may be appropriately applied. But education has no greater purpose than to prepare men to meet the shocks of life with the ability to keep their balance and not be swept away. Such ability can be gained by cultivating a wide acquaintance with the experience of the past as stored in poetic forms and thus ready to be relived in the imagination of the reader. From immediate realities intensely felt and vividly conveyed by poets down the ages we derive that broadening of sensibility and awareness of the nature of things that add up to wisdom. Only so can we achieve a measure of emotional stability in an unstable world. In a fine lyric Robert Frost has created an epitome of how the mature imagination responds to cataclysms.

> Not only sands and gravels
> Were once more on their travels,
> But gulping muddy gallons
> Great boulders off their balance
> Bumped heads together dully
> And started down the gully.
> Whole capes caked off in slices.
> I felt my standpoint shaken
> In the universal crisis.
> But with one step backward taken
> I saved myself from going.
> A world torn loose went by me.
> Then the rain stopped and the blowing
> And the sun came out to dry me.

The power to save oneself from going, whether by taking a backward step or a forward one, depends on vision. It is not pleasant to look at things we do not like, and Americans in particular have fallen into a self-indulgent way of closing their eyes to anything that does not please them. We have, to a marked degree, the ostrich habit. To learn to look steadily at our world, to realize the limitations of our powers, and to grasp the tragic implications of our destiny as men, we need now as always education by poetry. The "ancient fierce enigmas," as Whitman called them, are not to be dispelled by any rational analysis, but by imaginative preparation they may be faced with stoical courage or out-faced with mystical insight.

One of the early Puritan settlers in my part of the country used to declare that he never went to sleep without sweetening his mind with a morsel of Calvin. I cannot commend his choice of authors, but let us end by refreshing the imagination with a sonnet by Shakespeare, noticing in passing how the great poet goes immediately to the heart of the oldest of man's mortal difficulties.

> Poor soul, the center of my sinful earth,
> Thrall to these rebel powers that thee array,
> Why dost thou pine within and suffer dearth,
> Painting thy outward walls so costly gay?
> Why so large cost, having so short a lease,
> Dost thou upon thy fading mansion spend?
> Shall worms, inheritors of this excess,
> Eat up thy charge? Is this thy body's end?
>
> Then, soul, live thou upon thy servant's loss,
> And let that pine to aggravate thy store.
> Buy terms divine in selling hours of dross;
> Within be fed, without be rich no more;
> So shalt thou feed on Death, that feeds on men,
> For Death once dead, there's no more dying then.

Out for Stars:

A Meditation on Robert Frost[1]

STREAMLINING is one of the most popular fallacies of our time. If you apply streamlining to poetry the argument runs about as follows: Since the chief aim of poetry is to bring about a formal ordering or integration of the feelings, communication cannot be its main purpose. Consequently poetry that eliminates communication is purer, and hence better, than poetry that admits a "message." The poem should not attempt to rival the scientific textbook; or as Archibald MacLeish has so incisively put it, "A poem should not mean but be."

With the modernist poet's fastidious avoidance of meaning (once he has stated his *ars poetica*), it is instructive to compare the practice of a great poet like Dante, who seems curiously unaware of how much he might have improved

[1] First published in the *Atlantic Monthly* (May 1943).

his *Commedia* if he had not sought to use it as an instrument of communication. Instead of reducing the element of meaning to the lowest possible terms, Dante appears almost avid to multiply meanings, to double and redouble the implications of his thought. Can it be that disdain of meaning is a symptom of the poverty of poetry in a time of failing convictions?

A renewed perception of the many levels of implication beneath the innocent-looking surfaces of Robert Frost's poems reminded me recently of the manifold harmonies of Dante's great poetic instrument. Reading again in Mr. Untermeyer's expert selection, *Come In*, the lyric that so happily lends its title to the book, I became aware that the words of the poem were opening vistas in several directions, as from one spot in the forest the eye may fancy that it discerns colonnaded aisles leading off ahead, behind, and on either hand.

Particularly in the last two stanzas I thought I could detect an effect like "underpainting," layer upon layer, beneath the plain intent of the words:

> Far in the pillared dark
> Thrush music went—
> Almost like a call to come in
> To the dark and lament.
>
> But no, I was out for stars:
> I would not come in.
> I meant not even if asked,
> And I hadn't been.

Here is a poem which, though it does not shirk the obligation of lucid statement, is not exhausted when its surface

meaning has been communicated. Instead the simplicity
and clearness of the incident recorded leave the reader un-
impeded by verbal perplexities, not to turn away satisfied
unless he is a singularly obtuse reader, but to look further
into these limpid depths and perceive what he can, whether
of cloudy reflections of his own mind or of ultimate intentions lurking in the poet's.

After the labor of assimilating to our being much poetry
that aims not to mean but to be, the pleasure of encounter-
ing a poem that actually conveys a well-defined reading of
experience is enormous.

Taken literally, the lines I have quoted record a very ordinary incident of a walk at twilight. A man with an eye for
the first stars is distracted momentarily by the poignant
beauty of the thrush's song, but he refuses to follow its lure
into the darkening woods or to accept its mood of lamenta-
tion. The laconic last two lines confirm the New England
setting of the poem.

Indeed, the intonations are so characteristic that they
can hardly fail to recall to the many persons who have
listened to Robert Frost's remarkable readings from his
poems the voice of the poet himself. Every other part of
the poem is equally authentic. Much that Frost has written
attests his intimate acquaintance with country things: he
can be trusted to select the moment of the day when the
wood-thrush's song sounds clearest. His reference to stars
is no casual literary gesture, but a tribute to a lifelong passion for astronomy, amply confirmed in other poems.

Not only the person speaking, but the setting of the poem
is utterly true to life. It might be any one of the New Hampshire or Vermont farms where Frost has lived, since he has
seldom lodged far from the edge of the woods and the com-

panionship of trees. I do not know where this poem was written, or what landscape was present to the writer's mind, but to me it seems to fit perfectly the region of Ripton, Vermont, where he has latterly spent his summers.

The dark woods might be the half-mile stretch of state forest, largely pine, between his cottage on the Homer Noble place and "Iry" Dow's, the homeplace of his current venture in farming. To get from one property to the other by road is a matter of several miles, and it is natural, therefore, to cut through the woods. But if one were going nowhere in particular it would be easy to refuse the walk beneath the trees for a climb to upland pastures, whence as from a shelf hung high on the slope of the Green Mountains one may look off westward across a narrow strip of Lake Champlain to tumbled Adirondack masses on the rim of the world and above them the evening star.

Ripton is typical "Frost Country," though the bulk of his writing was done before he came to live in this neighborhood. It reached the height of its prosperity about the time of the Civil War. The mounting tide of human settlement then flowed up to the higher clearings; since then it has mostly receded, leaving behind a sparse population on "marginal" land and many cellar holes. Among the people are some whom Frost might name along with the best he has encountered anywhere in rural New England. Others are not to be clearly distinguished from the oddments on any beach at low tide.

There was "Iry" Dow, for example, now departed, who for upward of forty years professed to make his living as a blacksmith, though prevented by a weak heart from making any strenuous exertions. Consequently a great deal of conversation flowed between blows on the anvil. "That Iry

Dow," said one irritated customer, "is as much slower'n stock-still's stock-still is slower'n greased lightnin'." The year before he died, the village elected him to the legislature so that he might continue his endless talk without the bother of now and then pretending to beat on a horseshoe. Nothing that Frost found among these people would have suggested any need of revising what he had previously written of other little towns north of Boston.

The surrounding country, dominated by the ridge of the mountains, once partly settled, then unsettled again, is full of the wild things, both animals and plants, that the poet has so often observed and described. A great lover of woodlands and Morgan horses, the late Joseph Battell, once possessed much of Ripton, and his will is still reflected in the quantity of standing timber. So bold and numerous are the deer that vegetable gardens need the protection of an electrically charged wire. Overgrown roads follow the brooks and lead to abandoned mowings high on the ridges.

In one respect, however, Ripton is peculiar. It contains Bread Loaf, the summer school of English which Frost helped to found some twenty-five years ago and which he still benevolently frequents. Frost, in fact, would not be fully himself unless there were an educational project somewhere in the offing for him to cherish and humorously despair of, for he is a born teacher with a knack of charging dry subjects with intellectual excitement and a large patience for struggling learners.

Teaching to him is a natural extension of his unfeigned interest in people. I have seen him ask friendly, insistent questions about the little country town where a man was born and brought up, and have watched the man, at first answering with diffidence because for years he had been apologetic about his simple beginnings and anxious to live them down, gradually warm to his memories, discover a fresh respect for the sources of his being, and go out from the interview (as he said later) with a new dimension added to his personality. I doubt if Frost knew how much that conversation meant to the other man. He was just expressing an interest in the ways of little towns.

It is against the background of Ripton, then, that I picture Frost hearing thrush music, as it is there that I recall him in many other postures: a stocky figure but alert in motion, wearing an old suit and scuffed shoes, freshly laundered soft shirt open at his throat, his white hair tousled in the wind, his seafarer's blue eyes twinkling. One would find him skirting a mowing field, crossing a stone wall to a pasture where blueberries grew, measuring the water in the spring, or playing softball with young friends on a diamond wrung from the hayfield, where running for a fly was an adventure. Then would come hours of such converse as I never expect to repeat.

For me the poem I have quoted is inseparably bound up with these personal memories of the man and the region. But for anyone, even for anyone ages hence, it is marked with authentic traits of individuality, images to the ear and to the eye, that distinguish it from conventionalized writing just as readily as a portrait can be told from an idealized face when archaeologists study the sculptures found in the buried cities of Yucatan.

In the first instance, then, the poem is justified by its absolute integrity of substance. Whatever it speaks of is something that the poet has absorbed completely into himself, generally by seeing it, hearing it, living through it—less frequently by imaginative reading. But though the poem may appear simple and complete on the literal level, its texture may be dense with implied cross-references. In such poetry it is not inappropriate to look for undermeanings, at one's own risk, of course. The meanings may be all in the reader's eye, or again they may attain to a certain significance if they are confirmed by what the poet has elsewhere written.

Frost himself may be held responsible if readers persist in looking in his poems for more meaning than meets the casual eye. Though he denies a didactic intent, he is not unwilling to have his poetic records of experience flower in explicit apothegm. Only there is seldom or never any indication of his writing for the sake of the moral. In that respect he differs completely from makers of fables. La Fontaine, as Mr. Untermeyer claims, might conceivably have shaped the substance of Frost's "At Woodward's Gardens" into an apologue entitled "The Boy, the Monkeys, and the Burning-Glass," ending with the epigram: "It's knowing what to do with things that counts." But Frost's first instinct is to make sure of the reality of his material; nine-tenths of his poem is painstakingly devoted to picturing his monkeys, not as actors in a fable, but as actual monkeys. He calls our attention to their "purple little knuckles" and condenses all the confusion of the simian brain into one delicious line:

They bit the glass and listened for the flavor.

Not until that has been fully done does he turn to the moral as a means of rounding the poem. To call such a piece of writing a fable, as at least two good critics have recently chosen to do, is to label it as something less than it actually is. Except where Frost has completed his poem by attaching an abstract meaning to it—not necessarily a statement of the poem's whole meaning—he is entitled to insist that his intention has been to present, not the symbol of a thought, but an image of an experience. To this there is only one answer: that experience as Frost absorbs and interprets it often spreads out into so many ramifications that thoughts get tangled in it like stars seen through tree branches.

To consider now more searchingly the stanzas that I have quoted about the thrush, would it not be possible to read the episode as a literary parable? A poet of our time hears a birdlike voice from the dark wood (ancient symbol of error) singing of irremediable ills. The call to "come in to the dark and lament" awakens an impulse to become a modernist poet of the decadent school, to take the veil (or, as Frost once put it, "take the blanket") of calculated obscurity and imitate the fashionable lead of the French Symbolistes. The summons, however sweetly conveyed, can be resisted by a poet who has long considered it inappropriate "to write the Russian novel in America," and who prefers to keep on in the way he was going.

To place this interpretation on the poem (and I do not imply that the poem demands it) is to emphasize Frost's remarkable independence of the contemporary note in letters. Though he has studied the experimental poetry of recent years with attention—and some amusement—he has never felt called to share in any experiments except his own, which have been more far-reaching in their metrical subtlety than many readers realize. Ever since as a young poet barely out of his teens Frost was advised by a New York editor to try to write like Sidney Lanier, he has been set in his determination to write like no one but Robert Frost.

Out for Stars

His aloofness has been held against him. It has been asserted that any sensitive spirit of our time must be wounded by the spectacle of the world as it exists and must respond by exhibiting his mutilations in public. Frost's obvious cultivation of soundness and balance, therefore, has been taken as indicative of a refusal to face the bitter realities that really matter, of a retreat to a protected backwater safe from the storm. This to a man who, unlike many of his critics, has worked in the factory and on the farm, who has known poverty as well as grief, and who has waited twenty years for recognition of his work to overtake him!

If Frost has not been willing to come in to the dark and lament, it has not been because he was unacquainted with the night, but because he had something to do that pleased him better. Perhaps he has felt that the business of putting love in order, of creating form out of the formless, can be better done by a poet who declined to be warped by the pressures of modern living. At any rate he has been unwavering in his allegiance to an Emersonian conception of human wholeness.

His deep-seated instinct for centrality and balance brings us back to the poem of the thrush to discover its meaning as ethical symbol. We are not disappointed. What else does the poem portray but one of the familiar dilemmas of man's existence? His walk lies between the two extremes represented by the dark woods and the stars. To the heavenly extreme he can never attain, to the other he is unwilling to let himself descend, but he may be aware of both and may on occasion incline a little one way or the other. That is what our living is, discovering where the extremes lie and where we belong on a sort of scale drawn between them.

There are innumerable such scales in politics, in religion,

in education. If we do not complete the scale, we risk falling into the illusion of progress—that is, of supposing that we are drifting inevitably toward a far-off divine event—or we are conscious only of what we have fallen from and invent the myth of original sin. Looking toward one extreme only, we commonly speak of savagery in contrast to civilization. Frost recently made us aware of the other end of the scale when he declared, "The opposite of civilization is Utopia." Thus the scale is completed, and man is put back between the poles—where he belongs.

One result of thinking of the normal human position as somewhere midway between two extremes is to awaken a fierce distrust of extremists and totalitarians, no matter how high-minded they may be. Once we are forced as far as we can go toward either extreme, we are committed, we lose our power to maneuver, we must adopt the party line. Only from a central position can we be said to have the ability to choose that makes life dramatic. Frost would not trade the freedom of his material in the world as he finds it for any number of freedoms in Utopia. What he holds precious is the privilege of meeting the exigencies of life by apt recalls from past experience, with only enough newness to freshen thought.

But what if the world's crisis is so desperate as to justify a concerted movement to one extreme or the other in the attempt to alleviate it? Are we always to see life waste away into war, insanity, poverty, and crime and do nothing about it? Here indeed we touch on ultimate values. In an address to Amherst seniors a few years ago Frost declared that the thought of coming to condone the world's sorrow is terrible to contemplate. It is our darkest concern. Yet unless I mis-

Out for Stars

read the poem, Frost has indicated the inevitable response of a wise man in the poem we have been discussing. To be resolutely "out for stars" is not to be concerned overmuch with the still, sad music of humanity.

The poet must nerve himself to say with Housman, "Be still, my soul, and see injustice done." It is his function to realize the millennium, not in terms of social adjustments, but either

> right beside you book-like on the shelf,
> Or even better god-like in yourself.

Frost has spoken with deep compassion of the Shelleyan natures who insist on bearing their share, or more than their share, of the world's miseries, but he has not hesitated to proclaim that the call to struggle for society's betterment is "poetry's great anti-lure." He is not attracted by

> the tenderer-than-thou
> Collectivistic regimenting love
> With which the modern world is being swept.

The poet, in so far as he is a poet, must not be too cognizant of mankind's wounds or his own. His business is not to make humanity whole, but to explore the uses of wholeness. It is naïve to hang the class struggle on his shoulders. In the American tradition one does not have to join the army to be a good citizen.

If anyone still should ask, Why is the function that the poet performs so important that he may seek exemption from duties incumbent on his fellows? the best answer is, Read once again the lovely stanzas of "Come In" or the poem "Choose Something Like a Star" that stands as an afterword in the anthology of Frost's writings compiled by Mr. Untermeyer. Is it nothing to us that someone should be out for stars? Is it nothing in a universe where every star we can examine seems to be engaged in radiating incredible light and heat—is it nothing, in our preoccupation with war and wages and prices, to be reminded of the sense in which a star by its mere existence can "ask a little of us here"?

> It asks of us a certain height,
> So when at times the mob is swayed
> To carry praise or blame too far,
> We may choose something like a star
> To stay our minds on and be staid.

"Unit and Universe . . ." [1]

Literary allusion is a tricksy thing when it involves taste and judgment. Downright borrowing is another matter. Once the source of borrowed material has been found, there can be little further argument. But when an author embodies his admirations and dislikes in a blind reference, then the reader is faced with a new variety of the old game of "guess what I am thinking."

A neat instance of ambiguity occurs in a line from Robert Frost's A Masque of Reason, where the patriarch Job speaks of

> the way all things come round,
> Or of how rays return upon themselves,
> To quote the greatest Western poem yet.

[1] First published in Forum (July 1946).

Poetry and Civilization

What did Frost have in mind as "the greatest Western poem"? Probably many readers have asked the question without immediately arriving at an answer.

A professor at Williams who knows his Dante and who uses the word "western" in the scholarly sense of Western European culture, which includes American, recalled a passage in the *Paradiso* where Dante describes how a second or reflected ray constantly emerges from the first and bends back upon itself like a pilgrim who wishes to return. Could it be to this passage that Job's words pointed?

There would be no difficulty in accepting the *Divine Comedy* as a supremely great poem, but would a poet as firmly centered in the Western Hemisphere as Frost ever allude to anything east of Eastport, Maine, as "western"?

A professor from the University of Kansas City solved the puzzle by citing a line from Ralph Waldo Emerson's poem "Uriel":

> In vain produced, all rays return.

This was obviously what Frost was thinking of. But the solution of one question only raised another. In what sense could Emerson's lines possibly be designated as "the greatest Western poem yet"?

This question is unanswerable if we let ourselves suppose that the allusion is to be taken as a solemn critical pronouncement. It must not be regarded in that light at all. It is purely an expression of admiration. Emotion enters into it in the guise of the rhetorical figure known as hyperbole. Frost writes with a twinkle in his eyes. His intentions are not always to be read on the surface of his words. What he hopes to do here is to awaken his readers to the merits of a little masterpiece in our own literary tradition.

"Uriel" is a poem that grew directly out of intensely felt experience, as Emerson thought the truest poems should grow. It was not rooted in air. To understand it we must glance at its background in Emerson's biography.

Intellectuals of the 1830's were intoxicated by the vision that America afforded of new beginnings for the human race. Surely in an unpre-empted continent three thousand miles from their homelands men of European origin might slough off the errors and prejudices inherited from the past. Man might start afresh with good hope of realizing his best possibilities. This way of thinking, before it acquired the ponderous German label of Transcendentalism, was known simply as "the Newness." A leading Unitarian divine, the Reverend William Ellery Channing, set the tone of the movement when he exclaimed, "We cannot admit the thought that this country is to be only a repetition of the old world." Not long afterward Emerson in his first published book demanded, "Why should not we also enjoy an original relation to the universe?"

Inspired by this passion for new beginnings, Emerson urged American thinkers to learn from nature and from action rather than from the records of the past. "Books are for the scholar's idle times." The past lives only as it is incarnated in the present. The little world of Cambridge thrilled to the brave message.

But a year later, in 1838, Emerson spoke to the half dozen seniors of the Harvard Divinity School and earnestly begged them to find God in their own hearts rather than in sacred writ. Then the fat was in the fire. Every church, even the Unitarian, was solidly based on historical Christianity. Many of Emerson's hearers hastily concluded that in his zeal for what was fresh and immediate the speaker had

denied the divinity of Jesus. At once the faculty of the semi-
nary was up in arms. The Reverend Andrews Norton, breathing fire, denounced Emerson's address in an article entitled
"The Latest Form of Infidelity." Even the mild Henry
Ware, Jr., Emerson's friend and pastoral colleague, wrote
him a pained letter asking him to state the reasons for his
position. No reasons were given. Word went round New
England that a dangerous heretic had arisen. Emerson was
not asked to speak again at Harvard for thirty years.

Though he did not enter into controversy with his critics,
Emerson pondered over the meaning of his experience, ex-
tracting wisdom from what must have caused him real
suffering. When in 1847 his first volume of *Poems* was
published, it included a picture of what happens to an advanced thinker when he ventures to announce his eager
thought to a society comfortably bedded down in orthodox
beliefs. This was the fable of "the lapse of Uriel."

Emerson's generation would have immediately recognized
the symbol which holds the center of the poem. They were
brought up to parse Milton's *Paradise Lost* as meticulously
as they construed Virgil and Homer, and they would not
have failed to place Uriel as the archangel of the sun whom
Satan encountered as he approached God's newly created
world. Uriel, the personification of light, was an apt symbol
of intelligence, the light of the mind. Goethe's last words,
"Light, more light," have in our time become the motto of
a forward-looking party.

The setting of the poem is vaguely the Miltonic heaven
before the beginning of the world, or as Emerson put it, "or
ever the wild Time coined itself into calendar months and
days." When the poet wished to mention the supreme ruler
of heaven, however, he was at a loss to find a term that had

no previous religious connotations. He finally chose the Arabic word *Seyd,* meaning "the Lord."

Seyd, then, overheard the young inhabitants of paradise, as it might be the students of a divinity college, talking of everything under the sun and above it.

> The young deities discussed
> Laws of form and metre just,
> Orb, quintessence, and sunbeams,
> What subsisteth and what seems.

They were talking, in other words, about poetry, the laws of physics, and philosophy, the essences of things. Then Uriel, the original thinker, announced in all innocence a conception that upset the harmony of heaven: there is no such thing as a line. "Line in nature is not found."

A violent conservative reaction instantly flared up. The unheard of idea was immediately branded as treason, a menace to law and order.

> The stern old war gods shook their heads,
> The seraphs frowned from myrtle beds;
> Seemed to the holy festival
> The rash word boded ill to all.

(We are very close to the Harvard Divinity School in these lines.) The rash word of Uriel was straightway smothered under a conspiracy of silence. Nothing is easier than to close the eyes to unwelcome light.

So the discoverer of new truth was reviled and discredited, but the word once spoken lived on like an unextinguishable seed of fire. Once it had been pronounced, "truthspeaking things" reiterated it in spite of all that could be done to pervert and ignore their testimony. Uriel's voice was con-

firmed by astronomy, chemistry, physics, psychology, and
ethics. His thought echoed from the whole universe:

> And a blush tinged the upper sky,
> And the gods shook, they knew not why.

Is it only to Emerson that this fable applies, or to Galileo
before the Inquisition forced him to deny what his eyes had
seen, and to countless others whose bold and clear thought
has found no acceptance until long after the thinker was
dust? Socrates? Abelard?

Uriel's particular heresy was not just invented for purposes of the poem but was a basic idea in Emerson's own
philosophy. As always he felt that the laws of matter were
paralleled by the laws of mind, and hence his "sentiment"
that lines have no valid existence is stated doubly in terms
of both the outer and the inner worlds.

> Line in nature is not found;
> Unit and universe are round;
> In vain produced, all rays return;
> Evil will bless, and ice will burn.

Hardly twenty years ago an intelligent critic could refer
to "Uriel" as a "puzzle-poem." Its paradoxes, however, are
less cryptic than they seem. Outwardly considered, a mathematical line does not exist. It is only a concept in the mind.
What we see in nature are masses of greater or lesser extent.
Space, as physicists now tell us, is best thought of as curved.
Parallel lines converge if indefinitely prolonged, and a ray
shot out due north will eventually be found coming back
at us from the south. Air frozen solid will burn the skin as
effectively as red-hot iron.

Robert Frost, who is very unwilling himself to draw hard and fast lines between poets and men of science, has said that "Uriel" contains all of the philosophically sound and humanly relevant truth of Einstein's theory of relativity. It is indeed remarkable how this poem published in 1847 seems to anticipate the concepts that mathematical physics was to reach nearly a century later.

But Emerson is of his time, and of puritan New England, in placing emphasis on the ethical side of his doctrine. "Evil will bless." As a speculative thinker he was fascinated by the conception of dualities, day and night, hot and cold, good and evil. But the conviction that seemed to him most fundamental was the one which he stated in his essay on "Compensation," that opposites tend to merge and flow into each other. No rigid distinctions are possible. Experience is fluid and ultimately one. To the mind of Brahma, far and forgot are near, sunlight and shadow are the same.

This is a mystical and religious reading of life rather than a philosophical principle. It is not logical. But it was basic to Emerson.

Its ethical application can be very simply expressed in terms of a geographical figure. Suppose we regard the average man as morally in the longitude of 90 degrees west, or approximately at St. Louis, and that the meridian stands for him as the theoretical line that separates good and evil. His imagined good is west of him, in Denver and beyond; his imagined evil lies to the east . . . Pittsburgh . . . New York . . . Paris. The simplest way to attain the good is to move straight west. But it is also possible to attain the good by traveling east and keeping going. This has been the route followed by some of the greatest of the saints, who have passed through sin and evil till they emerged on the other side in confirmed holiness. The moral universe is round, and the lines drawn on it are as invisible as the meridians of longitude. Evil may prove to be only the long way round to good.

In his protest against a fixed pigeonholing of ethical values, Emerson was in full accord with the revolutionary temper of the early nineteenth century, when many received notions were being challenged and discarded. Shelley before him had been at some pains in *The Cenci* to construct a conceivable situation where a high-minded and resolute girl is driven to murder her father as the most moral solution of the hideous plot in which she finds herself enmeshed. The state, blindly following the pattern of ethical preconception, then proceeds to the judicial execution of the criminal while the church also condemns her as a sinner. Shelley's point like Emerson's is that no line can be drawn in advance. Before making a moral judgment every circumstance needs to be considered, and when that is done there is little to choose between one man and another. Shakespeare's Lear expressed the same thought when he pictured the self-righteous justice railing at the simple thief, and remarked, "change places, and, handy-dandy, which is the justice, which is the thief?" But he, of course, was mad.

Robert Browning, however, has enjoyed a reputation for sanity of an especially vigorous description. In *The Statue and the Bust* he tells of a noble duke and a high-born lady who have set their hearts on sin, but who postpone the carrying out of their intention to some more convenient time, which never comes. The poet remarks with something of Uriel's voice of cherub scorn that such technically virtuous souls "see not God, I know."

"Unit and Universe . . ."

And the sin I impute to each frustrate ghost
Is—the unlit lamp and the ungirt loin.

Salvation is dynamic. Evil will bless if one has the strength
to come out on the other side. Unit and universe are round.
Emerson's denial of the validity of lines in the moral
world, though somewhat advanced for the Cambridge of
a century ago, would no doubt seem quaintly irrelevant in
a modern psychopathic clinic. We have almost forgotten
the time when rigid ethical distinctions seemed important.
His radicalism on that side has no longer any target at
which to shoot. But just as Cambridge found his call for
an original relation to the universe an inspiring idea until
he disturbed deep-seated complacencies by giving it a religious application, so we can accept the conception that
"line in nature is not found" with indifference until it is
applied in the political world. Emerson himself did not
attempt to apply it there, and I very much doubt if Robert
Frost would sanction its extension in that direction.

But has the American political experiment any other
meaning than to show that the barriers between nations,
races, and   creeds are merely figures of speech, imaginary
lines established for convenience, temporary expedients
rather than eternal necessities? What is our melting pot but
a symbol of human unity, an assertion that essentially all
men are joined in a common destiny. One race . . . one
world . . . one fate. Unit and universe are round.

If there is a greater Western poem than that, where will
you find it?

Emily Dickinson

among the Victorians[1]

Iₙ ᴀᴛᴛᴇᴍᴘᴛɪɴɢ to estimate the literary heritage that was available to Emily Dickinson, Mr. R. P. Blackmur, in *The Expense of Greatness*, makes the following characterization of the language of poetry current in her time:

We can say, amiably enough, that the verse-language of mid-nineteenth century America was relatively nerveless, unsupple, flat in pattern, had very little absorptive power and showed no self-luxuriating power whatever. . . . The great estate of poetry as an available condition of language lay flat in a kind of desiccated hibernation, and the clue to resurrection was un-known.

[1] This lecture, the third of a series of six Percy Turnbull Memorial Lectures, was given at the Johns Hopkins University on January 14, 1947.

And he proceeds to observe that Whitman and Emily Dickinson, in revulsion from the desiccation, were obliged to rely entirely on their own natural aptitudes for language and hence never found satisfactory form, nor apparently were ever conscious of missing it.

But perhaps the case was not so desperate as Mr. Blackmur would make out. Rather than adopt an artificial and lifeless convention, Emily Dickinson sometimes compressed her notes for poems into a kind of grammatical shorthand of her own devising, or she let the words take the natural rhythms of speech without caring much about the pattern. This last is perhaps what Mr. Blackmur had in mind when he said that she was apparently not conscious of her lack of form. It would be truer to say that she fastidiously avoided perfunctory form. When we fix our attention, not on the confusing mass of poems finished and unfinished that her editors have indiscriminately huddled up together, but on the poems which presumably received her final approval, we are left with a new respect for her mastery of language and the inexhaustible variety and delicacy of her sense of form.

But Mr. Blackmur is right in maintaining that Emily Dickinson revolted from the literary standards to which her age paid deference. Indeed, her opposition is clear in her relations with Thomas Wentworth Higginson. She appealed to him to know if her verse were alive. He was not insensitive to such values, and apparently his reply helped to assure her. She said later in her hyperbolic way that it had saved her life. But he also hinted that her inspiration was wayward and that her rhymes observed no law. She quietly ignored his attempts to teach her, and he considerately desisted. This episode plainly shows that however uncertain she may have felt about the value of what she was writing she had no doubts at all about her literary method.

There is very little evidence to show that Emily Dickinson was aware that she was not alone in seeking more living forms of poetry than Victorian practice supplied. It is not even certain that she was consciously a rebel, since she was gifted with a profound and beautiful humility. But at the same time that she was willfully indulging herself in perfecting a sharp, astringent art of expression, other poets were independently seeking to escape from the confining standards of literary decorum. Mrs. Browning, for one, experimented with imperfect rhymes to see if she could not break down the conventions that she regarded as stifling. Emerson, Thoreau, Melville, and Whitman in this country were in various ways flouting the approved elegancies of poetry written for the drawing room. Thoreau, even more than Emily Dickinson, was disheartened by the abyss between his work and the sort of poetry that was currently successful, with the result that he impulsively burned much manuscript which he later wished he had saved.

Among the poets who reacted less violently against the accepted canons was Sidney Lanier, an interesting example of dissidence because his isolation as a southern writer of the Reconstruction Period gave him a certain perspective on the literary scene. In a letter of November 24, 1876, to Bayard Taylor, Lanier expressed his impatience with the feebleness of contemporary verse:

In looking around at the publications of the younger American poets, I am struck with the circumstance that none of them even attempt anything great. The morbid fear of doing something wrong or unpolished appears to have influenced their choice of subjects. Hence the endless multiplication of those little feeble magazine-lyrics which we all know; consisting of one minute idea, each, which is put in the last line of the fourth verse, the other three verses and three lines being mere sawdust and surplusage.

Lanier, who hoped himself to become a kind of John Keats with an American fiber, recognized the difficulty of making headway against the established expectation of smoothly finished verse. To his wife he spoke out, referring to his poem "My Two Springs":

Of course, since I have written it to print, I cannot make it such as I desire, in artistic design: for the *forms* of today require a certain trim smugness and clean-shaven propriety in the face and dress of a poem, and I must win a hearing by conforming in some degree to these tyrannies,—with a view to overturning them in the future.

Lanier's awareness of differences between what artistic integrity demanded and what it was possible to get into print throws a revealing light on Emily Dickinson's lifelong refusal to submit her poems to publication. She was not one to conform to "these tyrannies," and if the price to be paid for following her innermost convictions was lack of public recognition, she was willing to pay the price. But for poets in revolt against the stultifying restrictions of convention there was no common rallying point. They did their work in isolation without the support of knowing that others were working with them. Robert Frost could say of the fellow worker whose reverence for beauty he divined:

"Men work together," I told him from the heart,
"Whether they work together or apart."

Nevertheless those who have the courage to work apart must devote a certain amount of energy to overcoming the sense of utter loneliness. Generally they are thrown back upon the past and find support in establishing their kinship with the books and writers of other days.

Emily Dickinson was an eager reader. She formed numerous connections with sources of inspiration that made it unnecessary for her to rely entirely on her own aptitude for language while avoiding the stagnation of poetry in her time. The most obvious and sustaining of these influences was that of the Hebrew Bible, supplemented by Calvinistic theology, pulpit eloquence, and the verse of Dr. Watts and other writers of hymns. In her personal letters she often referred to poems by Tennyson, Lowell, and other secular poets as "hymns," and it would not be claiming too much to say that nine-tenths of her own poetry was written in meters made familiar to her by their use in the village hymnal. Some passages in her early correspondence likewise indicate that during her formative years Emily was not one who kept the Sabbath by staying at home, but that she attended church regularly and sometimes was profoundly stirred by the words spoken from the pulpit. Theological terms like election, grace, sacrament, and others were used in her poems with a nice sense of their technical meaning, while her fondness for religious imagery was constantly apparent. Unorthodox and unsettled she may have been in her religious convictions and affiliations, but she never outgrew the deep impression that her religious training had made upon her in childhood.

Most Victorian poets were men and women of religious nature, and their work is profoundly tinged with devoutness.

Among them Emily Dickinson occupies a special place because of her instinctive immediacy. Just as in her nature poems she is constantly aware of human implications, so in her religious lyrics she steadily brings the sacred to the level of the human. There is nothing that she respects more than her own soul. In her opinion God exists for man, not man for God. This is no doubt her central heresy. In its poetic consequences it meant that she could not force her mind to assume a "cosmic" point of view. She could sympathize with Moses or other Biblical characters as human beings, but she could not rouse herself to enthusiasm for the drama of salvation in general. Her first readers unconsciously felt the difference, and some of them resented it.

Browning's "Saul" may not unfairly be regarded as a typical Victorian handling of a large religious theme in terms of Biblical characters. The shepherd boy David, who is the narrator as well as the central actor in the poem, pictures the great warrior king of Israel sunk in irremediable melancholy and brooding. In his yearning to relieve the monarch of the shadow of death that weighs upon his spirit, David recognizes an intimation of God's infinitely greater love for His children and a foreshadowing of the divine willingness to atone by Christ's sacrifice for the sins of man. The poem ends with a splendid restatement of the mystery of Christ's incarnation. Throughout the poem the tone has been tender and reverent. Saul, though not one of the prophets, is notably exalted into a figure of heroic size, like a huge bronze statue moving.

Against the background of expectation indicated by Browning let us project one of Emily Dickinson's evocations of a Biblical personage.

Emily Dickinson

Belshazzar had a letter,—
He never had but one;
Belshazzar's correspondent
Concluded and begun
With that immortal copy
The conscience of us all
Can read without its glasses
On revelation's wall.

Somehow the story of the handwriting on the wall, which
seemed remote and mysterious in the Old Testament, has
become as familiar as the postman. Belshazzar is stripped
of his oriental splendors. He is merely a representative human being, standing for "the conscience of us all." He "had
a letter," just like you and me. And somehow, too, "Belshazzar's correspondent" has come to seem rather immediate.
Many people disliked having the trappings of reverence so
ruthlessly plucked away. One could read Browning with a
gentle glow of admiration, but this poem administered a
jolt. It was shocking, dangerous. It was Emily Dickinson.

Like everyone else, she read her Shakespeare. For her
Shakespeare was more than a great poet; the *Works* was a
unique book, the only book in the world. When she thought
that her eyes were failing, she consoled herself by the reflection that she could still listen to its lines read aloud. She may
have shared the romantic Victorian habit of regarding the
characters in the plays as real people indefinitely extensible
both backward and forward in time. She may have applied
moralistic standards in judging them. But evidence on these
points is not sufficient to be decisive. What is clearly manifest is that she learned from Shakespeare to treat language
with an imperial contempt for rule, exchanging the parts of

speech as convenience dictated, and sacrificing everything to the vitality of her thought. Resemblances to other poets may be noted, but there can be no doubt that Shakespeare provided her with the model that she studied most closely and absorbed most completely. There are echoes both of his cadences and of his conceits in her writing, but her main debt to him was not for literal borrowings. His liberal practice gave her the conception of language as a plastic medium to be shaped according to her desires. Moreover, her special fondness for *Othello* and *Antony and Cleopatra* indicates a certain maturity in her affection. These are not the plays that would be chosen by one who liked Shakespeare prettified. Emily Dickinson turned to him as one genuine craftsman to another.

Her relations with Donne, Herbert, Vaughan, and other seventeenth-century religious poets are curiously blank. One would suppose that she would have delighted in them, in spite of the fact that they were at the time out of fashion, except as Herbert was perennially read by pious people. It is disconcerting to find that she never referred to Donne at all or gave any indication that she was aware of his work. Vaughan's name she did know, though somewhat uncertainly since she misspelled it, and the one quotation she made from him toward the end of her life came from a poem frequently included in the anthologies. We would not be sure that she had ever seen Herbert's poems if two stanzas from his "Matins" had not survived in her handwriting. Nothing of Crashaw, nothing of Andrew Marvell. If she had lived a generation later, she would almost certainly have discovered her temperamental affinity with these poets. As it was, she recognized the genius of Sir Thomas Browne and once or twice assimilated to her poetry a phrase that may have been taken from him, but she leaves us in doubt concerning her awareness of his contemporaries. In general it may be said, however, that Emily Dickinson read far more than we can now prove that she read.

Early reviews of Emily Dickinson's poems, perhaps prompted by a remark of Higginson's, saw in her work "a distant echo of Blake," but we have no assurance that she had ever read anything of his. In all probability very few of his poems were available in Amherst until Emily was more than halfway through her span of life. Robert Burns, on the other hand, she certainly knew and in her very early poems sometimes imitated. But except for the few phrases that betray her girlish susceptibility to the sentimental warmth of Scottish song, it is difficult to establish any connection between Emily Dickinson and the British poets of the Romantic Movement. Her nature poems, as we have seen, are cast in a different mold from Wordsworth's, her love poems have nothing in common with Shelley's. Coleridge, Scott, and Byron, though she knew some of their work, inhabit another world from hers. Superficially it might be supposed that Landor, the master of graceful and polished epigram, might resemble her more closely than any other early-nineteenth-century poet. But Landor, as a devoted student of the classics, wrote by the book, whereas Emily Dickinson forged her epigrams in the white heat of her eager heart. The difference between them is the difference between the stately communication of men and women in the drawing room and the soul-to-soul communings that occur upstairs.

At the name of Keats, however, we must pause for a moment's consideration. When Higginson, in 1862, asked her about her reading, she replied surprisingly that for poets she had Keats and the two Brownings. At first glance her mention of Keats would seem to furnish an example of her paradoxical fondness for a writer whose work stands at the opposite pole from hers. The art of Keats was an art of invention and expansion, an effort to "load every rift with ore." Her art was one of ultimate compression, a defining of limits, a refining of the thrice refined. Yet if one looks closely at Emily Dickinson's poems one can imagine that he sees traces of Keatsian influence, though rarely among her most characteristic pieces. It is unusual to find her in an expansive moment, but a few love poems written presumably before her catastrophe of frustration have a certain amplitude and even a sensuous delight in piling detail on detail that is almost Keatslike.

> I tend my flowers for thee,
> Bright Absentee!
> My fuchsia's coral seams
> Rip, while the sower dreams.
>
> Geraniums tint and spot,
> Low daisies dot,
> My cactus splits a beard
> To show its throat.
>
> Carnations tip their spice
> And bees pick up.
> A hyacinth I hid
> Puts out a ruffled head,
> And odors fall
> From flasks so small
> You marvel how they held.

Emily Dickinson

Globe roses break
Their satin flake
Upon my garden floor,
Yet Thou not there—
I had as lief they bore
No crimson more. . . .

For what it may be worth, here is a somewhat similar
passage in Keats's more sedate measure:

Thou shalt, at one glance, behold
The daisy and the marigold;
White-pluméd lilies, and the first
Hedge-grown primrose that hath burst;
Shaded hyacinth, alway
Sapphire queen of the mid-May;
And every leaf and every flower
Pearléd with the self-same shower.

Recent investigation of Keats in the light of theories
about the association of ideas that were current in his time
has emphasized the experimental quality of certain of his
early poems, in which he seems to be recording chance se-
quences of images that flowed through his mind in states
of revery or daydreaming. Emily Dickinson likewise wrote
a few poems in which she appears to be reproducing the
motions of a mind either actually dreaming or dominated
by waking fancy. The strange poem beginning, "In winter
in my room," which describes the transformation of a
mysterious small worm into a pursuing serpent of hideous
power, concludes with the significant words, "This was a
dream." It could easily be given a Freudian interpretation,
but not by me. Other poems, such as "I know some lonely

houses off the road," and "I started early, took my dog,"
have elements of unreality about them which suggest that
they too belong with such dream-inspired compositions as
"Kubla Khan." One wonders whether Emily Dickinson,
like Keats, was tempted by the example of Coleridge to

> let wingéd Fancy wander
> Through the thought still spread beyond her:
> Open wide the mind's cage-door
> She'll dart forth, and cloudward soar.
> O sweet Fancy! let her loose. . . .

The effect is in any case very much the same as that of a
succession of images, real and imaginary, mingled, combined in a structure reared half automatically by the mind
and given little intentional shaping. Mr. Yvor Winters has
suggested that in the following poem the sea should be
identified with death, as in Whitman's "Out of the Cradle
Endlessly Rocking," where the identification is explicitly
stated. Whether his idea is accepted or not, the poem clearly
resembles a dream and might be similarly interpreted.

> I started early, took my dog,
> And visited the sea;
> The mermaids in the basement
> Came out to look at me,
>
> And frigates in the upper floor
> Extended hempen hands,
> Presuming me to be a mouse
> Aground, upon the sands.
>
> But no man moved me till the tide
> Went past my simple shoe,

And past my apron and my belt
And past my bodice too,

And made as he would eat me up
As wholly as a dew
Upon a dandelion's sleeve—
And then I started too.

And he—he followed close behind;
I felt his silver heel
Upon my ankle,—then my shoes
Would overflow with pearl.

Until we met the solid town,
No man he seemed to know;
Then bowing with a mighty look
At me, the sea withdrew.

With the Keats of "The Eve of St. Agnes" and "Hyperion" Emily Dickinson has nothing in common, but there are tantalizing parallels between her work and some aspects of Keats's odes. His psychological observation of the close relationship of melancholy and ecstatic delight in the "Ode to Melancholy" is akin to the discernment which prompted her to write:

For each ecstatic instant
We must an anguish pay
In keen and quivering ratio
To the ecstasy.

The famous identification of Beauty and Truth at the end of the "Ode on a Grecian Urn" must have been in Emily Dickinson's mind when she wrote a lyrical statement of the same identity. It was characteristic of her passion for im-

mediacy that she translated Keats's abstractions into terms
of human figures.

> I died for beauty, but was scarce
> Adjusted in the tomb,
> When one who died for truth was lain
> In an adjoining room.
>
> He questioned softly why I failed?
> "For beauty," I replied.
> "And I for truth,—the two are one;
> We brethren are," he said.
>
> And so, as kinsmen met a night,
> We talked between the rooms,
> Until the moss had reached our lips,
> And covered up our names.

Nothing in Keats can quite match the eerie imagination of
the last stanza, but in other respects the two poets have
something in common. Even the sensuously luxuriating
Keats who transcribed the blaze of sunset in the magic lines

> While barréd clouds bloom the soft-dying day,
> And touch the stubble-plains with rosy hue,

has an ethereal counterpart in the Emily who saw from her
window

> How the old mountains drip with sunset,
> How the hemlocks burn!
> How the dun brake is tipped with tinsel
> By the wizard sun!

and who could picture the clouds of another sunset as

> Blazing in gold and quenching in purple,
> Leaping like leopards to the sky.

Even Keats, who loved "lucent syrops tinct with cinnamon," could not cherish the names of gems more caressingly than this puritan spinster.

The leading British poets who were her own contemporaries Emily Dickinson absorbed with passionate admiration. Toward Elizabeth Barrett Browning indeed she became almost an idolater, reading everything she wrote and greeting the final collection of her poems with a lyric eulogy beginning,

> Her "Last Poems"—
> Poets ended.

From traveled friends Emily eagerly collected all they could tell her about the Brownings' menage in Florence. Robert Browning too she fairly worshiped and Tennyson she could quote largely without book. Yet there is hardly a trace of these poets in her own writing. Her poetry, she realized, was not of the same kind as theirs. She supposed, it would seem, that the advantage lay entirely with them. Were they not authors who had won universal public esteem? For herself she hoped not to be considered "the only kangaroo among the beauty," but she could not be sure of the value of her achievement. With rare persistence, nevertheless, she continued to write according to her own system, resisting all Higginson's well-meant efforts to bring her to conformity with Victorian standards.

As compared with the run of poets of the Victorian era, both British and American, Emily Dickinson lives in an atmosphere charged with ozone. She belongs with the small group of writers whose prose or verse was dictated by an overwhelming need of compensatory exertion. The act of creation for her was a purgative action, an aesthetic response to a psychological compulsion. Emily Brontë, Melville, and

Dostoievski were of the same type. Tennyson and Browning, Longfellow and Lowell, were of a different order.

To the sometimes overexalted and overstrained sentiment
of Victorian poets Emily Dickinson opposed a cool apprais-
ing exactitude of vision. She did not attempt to disguise
reality by lapping it in rhetoric. Browning might in a moment of exuberant optimism place a spirited glorification
of old age in the mouth of his Rabbi Ben Ezra:

> Grow old along with me!
> The best is yet to be,
> The last of life for which the first was made.

But Emily had no illusions about the old. She tended a bed-
ridden mother for seven years. Moreover she had used her
own unsparing eyes.

> That odd old man is dead a year,
> We miss his stated hat;
> 'Twas such an evening bright and stiff
> His faded lamp went out.
>
> Who miss his antiquated wick?
> Are any hoar for him?
> Waits any indurated mate
> His wrinkled coming home?
>
> Oh, life, begun in fluent blood
> And consummated dull!
> Achievement contemplating this
> Feels transitive and cool.

No "festal board, lamp's flash, and trumpet's peal" in the
dim decline of old age as far as Emily could see.

Tennyson in the first flush of Victorian enthusiasm for

56

the chivalric symbol of "self-reverence, self-knowledge, self-control" could write the slightly ridiculous lines on Sir Galahad:

> My good blade carves the casques of men,
> My tough lance thrusteth sure.
> My strength is as the strength of ten
> Because my heart is pure.

Emily Dickinson, on the contrary, was impressed by the dearth of miracles in this earthly life.

> I took my power in my hand
> And went against the world;
> 'Twas not as much as David had,
> But I was twice as bold.
>
> I aimed my pebble, but myself
> Was all the one that fell.
> Was it Goliath was too large,
> Or only I too small?

Or to bring out the difference still further, compare the poetic strategy that Tennyson employed in *In Memoriam* with Emily Dickinson's dealings with death and bereavement in well over two hundred brief poems. Tennyson finely expresses the shock of personal loss, but turns from man's inner world to seek from God and Nature some answer to the dark riddle of mortality. None is forthcoming, for the simple reason that the questions Tennyson poses are not genuine questions at all, but merely demands for emotional reassurance. In the end he relapses upon the rather lame solution that in the course of time the pang of sorrow is dulled and the scheme of things is somehow to be trusted. Emily Dickinson, with a salutary instinct for what

57

is appropriate, never asks any cosmic questions, but focuses her attention steadily on the meaning of death to the individual soul. It is true that

> Parting is all we know of heaven,
> And all we need of hell.

But death, considered with the intensity of her microscopic gaze, at length yields its own antidote. In physical extinction she discovers the source of spiritual vitality here and now. Without shifting ground or evading the issue, she has reached through "the admirations and contempts of time" to the stability of "the Finite furnished with the Infinite."

In this respect the quality of Emily Dickinson's vision seems to me remarkably like that of Dostoievski. In a study of his fiction Professor Janko Lavrin has written:

A very intensive kind of realism can be obtained by concentrating on man's inner world. It results in the psychological novel in which a religious-philosophic quest merges with "psychology" to such an extent as to become one with it. A quest of this kind frequently represents the author's own inner travail—exteriorized and projected into human characters whose "philosophy" is not a matter of intellect only, but of what might be called one's total inner experience.

Emily Dickinson, since she was not writing novels, seldom projected her thoughts in terms of characters, but she did exteriorize and personify "ideas-emotions" or "ideas-forces," which people, as in a morality play, the stage of her soul. The drama there enacted is a chaotic and often unresolved clash of opposing principles, as in life itself, but she does not let the play end in ruin and the victory of the Conqueror Worm. For her dramatic insights she found the brief lyric a suitable vehicle. A Melville or a Dostoievski might employ a novel, a Pascal or a Nietzsche an aphorism. It is not without significance that many of Emily's poems are aphoristic.

She has been called, I think not very perceptively, a feminine Walt Whitman. We may appropriately close this series of comparisons, therefore, with a short examination of her likenesses and unlikenesses to her great American contemporary. They are alike, as has already been pointed out, in their revulsion from the deadness of mid-century poetry, but on the positive side they have little in common. Whitman's loose democracy, his easygoing assimilation of the crowd, is as different as possible from Emily Dickinson's prim distaste for humanity in the mass.

> The popular Heart is a cannon first,
> Subsequent a drum;
> Bells for an auxiliary
> And an afterward of rum.

Their distinctive attitudes emerge rather sharply if we read in close conjunction a well-known poem by each on the spider. Whitman writes:

> A noiseless, patient spider,
> I mark'd, where, on a little promontory it stood, isolated;
> Mark'd how, to explore the vacant, vast surrounding,
> It launch'd forth filament, filament, filament, out of itself;
> Ever unreeling them—ever tirelessly speeding them.
>
> And you, O my Soul, where you stand,
> Surrounded, surrounded, in measureless oceans of space,
> Ceaselessly musing, venturing, throwing,—seeking the
>   spheres, to connect them;

Till the bridge you will need be form'd—till the ductile
  anchor hold;
Till the gossamer thread you fling, catch somewhere, O my
  Soul.

By avoiding conventional cadences Whitman has here
freshened what is in essence a well-worn device—the cou-
pling of a physical object with a moral or spiritual analogy.
His poem is built on the same plan as Bryant's "To a Water-
fowl" and Longfellow's "The Village Blacksmith," but the
poet's reputation for daring originality and his employment
of free verse have disguised the commonplace and outworn
mode of thought. Against a background of Whitman's more
oratorical chants this piece has the effect of a few words
spoken in a quiet conversational tone by a man engaged in
making a soapbox speech.

Emily Dickinson wrote several poems on spiders. In the
one I am quoting she, like Whitman, was pointing her observations at humanity while seeming to speak of the spider.

> The spider as an artist
>   Has never been employed,
> Though his surpassing merit
>   Is freely certified
>
> By every broom and Bridget
>   Throughout a Christian land.
> Neglected son of genius,
>   I take thee by the hand.

Do not be misled by the ironic ending into thinking that
this poem is a sentimental assertion of sympathy for the
least of God's creatures. It is nothing of the sort. Emily
Dickinson is making an assertion that James McNeill Whis-

tler would have delighted to underscore, namely that artistic merit is certified by the hostility of the vulgar. And what is the "Christian land" where works of genius are brushed off as any housemaid might treat a spiderweb? Is there a suspicion that it could be none other than New England? It is easy to suggest parallels for Whitman's poem, but where else in American literature can we find the like of Emily Dickinson's lambent intellectual satire?

No one tradition can account for Emily Dickinson. Her language is drawn from the Bible and Shakespeare, but likewise from the *Springfield Republican* and Webster's *American Dictionary*. She translates Calvinistic theology into household metaphor and expresses profound psychological insights in the locutions of daily speech. Her transcendental flights never get so far from the ground that they cannot be punctured by fact. Emerson and Yankee humor are blended in her composition.

She stands as a precursor of the modern mind, whom we have not yet fully overtaken. Born seven years before Queen Victoria came to the throne, and brought up to read Tennyson, Browning, Dickens, the Brontës, and George Eliot with transports of appreciation, Emily nevertheless miraculously freed herself from Victorian trammels when she came to write her tiny lyric notations on life. Her novel aim was to find words for the stark integrity of her inner and outer experiences. At a time when everything from the village blacksmith to the chambered nautilus was tagged with an ethical message, Emily believed that a hummingbird, a snake, a mushroom, or a blade of grass was poem enough if she could only get it on her page. With equal honesty she set down her devastating observations of people, her alternations of doubt and faith, her longing for high companionship, her agony of renunciation, and her constant awareness of the creeping shadow of death. Hers was an essentially modern spirit, learning, as we have not yet fully learned, to make the best of a world that has undergone an intellectual fragmentation bombing.

Pursuit of the Overtakeless[1]

As the train from Washington reached the outskirts of Philadelphia, I was thinking of Emily Dickinson, who with momentous consequences to herself had made this same journey some eighty years before. Philadelphia was the city, according to the highly colored story given out by her niece, where she first met the preacher whose spirit answered to her own—

Mine, here in vision and in veto!

—but who could not be hers in fact because he was already married. Out of her thwarted longing for companionship with the adored clergyman came a lyric outpouring which included the most intensely moving love poems ever written by an American poet.

Emily Dickinson's biography was badly in need of clari-

[1] First printed in the *Nation* (July 2, 1949).

fication. How far did her romance, described by her niece as "Plutonic," have a basis in fact?

I gave myself to him,
And took himself for pay . . .

Surely, not to be taken literally. But on the other hand, could her poems with specific details of time, place, and action be considered nothing more than dramatizations of a devotion never openly confessed? These were questions which I was concerned to solve.

Toward the end of her life Emily Dickinson referred to the Reverend Charles Wadsworth, formerly pastor of the Arch Street Presbyterian Church, as "my dearest earthly friend" and applied to him a line from Tennyson: "Of love that never found its earthly close, what sequel?" Was he, then, to be identified with the "lover" of her poems?

Behold the atom I preferred
To all the lists of clay!

And if so, was she assured of his response, or was she merely finding relief in letting her fancy create a dream of wish fulfillment? The revelations swathed in reticence which the Dickinson family had vouchsafed were inconclusive and contradictory. It occurred to me that Wadsworth's younger son lived in Philadelphia. What could he tell me of his father's friendship with Miss Emily Dickinson of Amherst? On the impulse I left the train to seek him out.

The telephone book listed him as a doctor and gave me the address of his office. I walked the few blocks from Broad Street and found myself in front of a massive stone building, a brass plate beside the door. It was the Philadelphia Morgue, Dr. William S. Wadsworth, Coroner.

Pursuit of the Overtakeless

Dropped into the
Ether Acre!
Wearing the sod gown—

The freshness of the April afternoon did not follow me
through the heavy doors. Inside was a pervasive, timeless
sensation of disinfectants. An attendant took my name and
returned with word that Dr. Wadsworth would see me as
soon as he had finished with a family who had called to
identify a corpse. I sat in the waiting-room.

Because I could not stop for Death,
He kindly stopped for me . . .

A forlorn group of three filed out. Behind them came a
tall erect figure of a man with graying hair and strongly
lined face. My underthought at first glimpse of him was
that I had seen someone like him somewhere, but the resemblance was too vague to trace. I explained my interest
in Emily Dickinson, and the doctor gravely led the way to
his office up a flight of stairs and along a corridor. The passage was lined with glass-fronted cases crowded with dirks,
revolvers, razors, blackjacks, bits of rope, kits of tools, rifles,
and sawed-off shotguns. I realized that this was the munici-
pal collection which reporters like to call the "chamber of
horrors."

In a comfortable room fitted up with a large desk, book-
cases, and easy chairs but still keeping a faint odor of
formaldehyde, the doctor lighted the first of a succession
of stogies. Through the open door at my right I was conscious of the gleam from the brass handle of a particularly
murderous stiletto.

One need not be a chamber to be haunted . . .

65

Poetry and Civilization

I asked a few casual questions, knowing the answers, to test the reliability of my informant. Dr. Wadsworth talked with animation and with occasional bursts of dramatic intensity breaking through his reserve. He spoke of his father's lifework as an evangelist whose sermons, though always quietly delivered, exercised an electric influence on his congregation and with their fervent urgency disarmed the impenitent. Each one mounted to a compelling climax in sheer eloquence of conviction.

> Deals one imperial thunderbolt
> That scalps your naked soul.

Charles Wadsworth was a man of intense sympathies, impatient of routine, who would cross the street to escape a trivial encounter but was unsparing of himself in his ministrations to the sick and to all afflicted and troubled spirits.

"People clung to him," said the doctor.

"Was Emily Dickinson one?"

He made a slight bow of assent.

"How did your father happen to call on her in Amherst? He had some reason to be in that locality?"

> There came a day at summer's full
> Entirely for me . . .

"His intimate friend James Clark lived in Northampton. He sometimes visited there. I suppose it is not far to Amherst, and his kindliness prompted him to pay a parochial call—on a distant parishioner. Miss Dickinson may have written to ask him for comfort. So many people needed him."

> I got so I could stir the box
> In which his letters grew . . .

66

"He would not have preserved such letters?"

A decided negative.

The picture that emerged, as we talked through an hour, was that of a man utterly consecrated to his ministry, happily married and devoted to his family, finding complete fulfillment of his marvelous power to uphold and strengthen the wavering souls of his flock. In such a career there was not the slightest room for a wayward inclination. One could see how Emily Dickinson might idolize such a man, but what could she have meant to him?

"Did your father ever speak of Emily Dickinson's poems?"

"He would not have cared for them. The poetry he admired was of a different order. He wrote poems himself when he was a young man. You see he came of a family, I think the only family, that has given to the world two poets of the first rank."

"Henry Wadsworth Longfellow, of course, and—?"

"William Wordsworth. Wadsworth and Wordsworth are variant spellings of the same family name."

It came to me in a flash that the man before me was the image of Wordsworth in old age, the same craggy north-of-England face.

"My father was not one," he was saying, "to be unduly impressed by a hysterical young woman's ravings."

> *Capacity to terminate*
> *Is a specific grace.*

Once more I ran the gauntlet of lethal weapons and breathed with relief a freer air. It seemed that my question had been laid to rest.

A College Graduate's Reading [1]

SOME of you are just casu-
ally passing through the year 1928, but to others of us it will
retain a peculiar and lasting significance. Through your invitation—an honor of which I am deeply sensible—I am
privileged this morning to extend to you, my fellow classmates, on behalf of the faculty our best wishes for your future as Amherst alumni. These farewells spoken here in the
bosom of our college family may seem a little premature,
since we have not yet quite done with you as undergraduates.
The official and public ceremonies of separation are still
to be achieved. But it is appropriate to begin to say farewell
at this final Chapel exercise, for we trust that as you pass
out for the last time as a senior class, you will feel that you
are leaving behind the most intimate and familiar part of

[1] An address given at the Senior Chapel exercises of the Class of
1928.

Amherst, its inner shrine and penetralia, its spiritual home. Perhaps to many of you now the thought of Chapel will remind you of home only as "the place where, when you have to go there, they have to take you in." But in time, and I trust soon, as you review your college memories, the moments spent in this room may come to seem "something you somehow hadn't to deserve" and so will fulfill the gentler meaning of home.

Since I am addressing particularly a group whose members may, according to our hopes and expectations, rise to positions of influence in church or school, or of affluence in business, industry, law, or politics, I find it hard to resist the temptation to use the time at my disposal for perfecting the education which you have been undergoing during the past four years. May I just insinuate the hope that your early struggles in whatever walk of life you select may see the sloughing off of the habit (if you have it) of writing the word "together" with a hyphen and the possessive case of the pronoun "it" with an apostrophe; that your first marked successes in your chosen field may be accompanied by a conviction that the phrase "due to" must always be anchored to a noun; and that finally, when you arrive at the presidency of rotary club, bank, chamber of commerce, bar association, masonic lodge, medical association, college, corporation, or nation, the climax of your career may be illuminated by the dawn of a distinction between the uses of "shall" and "will"? And now that I have eased my professional conscience by suggesting the discontinuance of certain collegiate habits, let me consider with you for a few moments the extension into later life of one of the habits acquired in college which may well be continued—the habit of disinterested reading.

I would speak to you now, not as teacher to students, but

as a confirmed reader of books to others potentially devoted.
And as a motto for my discourse I should like to repeat after
the father of English poets, Geoffrey Chaucer, a few lines as
appropriate today as they were five hundred years ago,
though their language must be freshened for our comprehension:

> And as for me, though that I konne but lyte,
> On bokes for to rede I me delyte,
> And to hem yive I feyth and ful credence,
> And in myn herte have hem in reverence
> So hertely, that there is game noon
> That fro my bokes maketh me to goon,
> But yt be seldom on the holyday;
> Save certainly, whan that the monethe of May
> Is comen, and that I here the foules synge,
> And that the floures gonnen for to sprynge,
> Fairwel my boke and my devocioun.

Possibly some of you will feel most in sympathy with the
last line of this passage. The month of May is upon us.
Within two weeks you may all say, "Farewell my book," and
perhaps in respect to serious reading lead a life that is henceforth a perpetual May. Many of you will never again be told
to read a book with even the slight persuasiveness that a
college instructor can exercise. Am I wrong in suspecting
that the prospect is not altogether void of consolation?

You will all continue to read, of course; that is almost a
biological necessity. But the companionate marriage with
things of the mind contracted in college may easily be termi-
nated at graduation. The college graduate, solicited on every
hand by offers of cheap aesthetic and intellectual satisfactions, is too often content to satisfy his lust for reading with

the common journals of the street, diversified perhaps by a little philandering with the *American Mercury* or a casual flirtation with such literary light o' loves as the latest book of the month. This is the easy course. To contract with great books a permanent wedlock, a lifelong companionship with the prospect of intellectual offspring, is not an easy thing. A man's time is rarely at his own disposal. It takes effort, planning, and self-denial to save out of a busy day even as much as fifty minutes for serious reading. Moreover, it is particularly hard to continue a habit of reading for its own sake in the first few years after a college course. You leave the classroom somewhat jaded and stuffed with reading. What you have absorbed will last you for five or ten years, and the danger of ending with a mind unexercised and un-breathed does not seem very immediate. Meanwhile the distractions of a change of life are to be faced. Thus it is that many men become flabby readers in the decade follow-ing college and are never again able to get into training.

Now I am not going to urge upon you the pleasure of read-ing. That is commonly too much spoken of. The enjoyment of books may indeed be one of the greatest pleasures of life, but it is properly a by-product, not an end, of reading. The spirit in which reading should be approached may be expressed in a remark I once overheard in our swimming pool addressed to a hesitating diver by the Neptune of those regions. It was: "Come on. Get your dive, and never mind if it hurts you." To the man who has plunged deep and successfully mastered a difficult book is reserved a joy that only the athlete and the sportsman can share. But it is a plain fact that a great book cannot be read by a mind that has "gone soft." A soft mind reads merely for the sake of amusement, with the intention of getting through as

soon as possible, and ends the book in much the same condition as it began. A confirmed reader, on the contrary,
rejoices as a strong man to run a race in the demands that
his author makes upon him. He delights in exercising,
strengthening, and enriching the various faculties of his
mind and will stay with a difficult book until he has absorbed
into himself all the concentrated experience that it has to
offer. The attitude of an athletic-minded reader toward
books may be illustrated by an anecdote of the great literary
hammer-thrower of the eighteenth century, Dr. Samuel
Johnson. When he and his satellite were traveling in the
Hebrides, Boswell discovered that the only book in his
companion's luggage was a copy of Cocker's *Arithmetic*.
On his expressing surprise at the Doctor's choice of a book
to travel with, Johnson replied: "Why, Sir, if you are to
have but one book with you upon a journey, let it be a book
of science. When you have read through a book of entertainment, you know it, and it can do no more for you; but a
book of science is inexhaustible." If I could wish you any
lasting benefit as a result of your investment in the College and the College's investment in you, it would be that
you become confirmed readers of inexhaustible books,
whether of science or of the imagination.

There is, I think, more reason now than formerly why you
should steep yourselves in the great classics at least of your
own tongue; and at the same time there is less certainty
than ever before that you will do so. Many voices will urge
you to fall in with the tendencies of the time: to read works
of popular enlightenment in order to keep informed of the
scientific discoveries of the moment; to study only that
much of the story of philosophy as may be epitomized in
words comprehensible to a child of eight; to triumph over

the great names of the past with the assumed superiority of ephemeral biographers; and to live with recent poetry and fiction because such writing most clearly mirrors the problems, hopes, needs, and despairs of our own day. Something, of course, may be said in favor of such a program, and I should be tempted to say it if I felt that there was any danger of your neglecting current books. But, on the whole, it seems to me that a finer use of reading lies in re-enforcing those qualities which we do not inevitably and as a matter of course acquire; in bringing us face to face with attitudes which are not the commonplaces of our everyday experience; and so in compensating for the unbalance to which our provincial situation in time exposes us. We cannot avoid being men of our own age, but we can if we choose also acquire some status as citizens of the larger segment of eternity comprehended in the whole recorded literature of our race.

Nearly every age known to us has its characteristic virtues and defects, and if in reference to our own times I speak of two weaknesses or failings against which our reading may guard us, let it not be thought that I am insensible to modern virtues. A certain patriotism in time is as becoming as patriotism of locality. I am glad to be a child of this age, to share as I may in its hopes and achievements. Even its shortcomings I prefer to the vices and brutalities of some other historical periods. The two failings that I am about to mention are, at least, the defects of qualities that I would not have us be without.

In the advancement of science and in the extension of its applications to the physical world have been won some of the most remarkable triumphs of the last century. We say, therefore, with some complacency that we are living in a scientific age. But unfortunately this does not mean that we are all scientific in our attitude. It means merely that all of us enjoy the benefits of applied science, most of us have our thinking colored by pseudo-science, and a very few of us become competent to follow the exacting pursuit of pure science. Those of us who are not engaged in the actual work of science are particularly liable to become victims of its misinterpretations. Just as every great religion has sooner or later become encrusted with a mythology, so positive science has been warped and distorted by its camp-followers and fuglemen to satisfy simple and literal minds, hot for certainties, who can no more understand the patient skepticism of the true scientist than they can comprehend the infinite vision of the religious mystic. Science, in plain terms, is developing its own mythology. If you want an illustration, ask any competent biologist to tell you what is positively known about the process whereby inorganic matter becomes, or became, living protoplasm, and then read the early chapters of Mr. H. G. Wells's *History of the World.* You will find there as pretty a creation-myth as any in the Book of Genesis. However, if you prefer Mr. Wells's unicellular organism engendered by sunlight from the green slime of the sea to Adam and Eve, or the cave man to Jonah and the whale, or the luminiferous ether to the Virgin, it does not much matter. If the contest were simply between the mythology of science and the mythology of religion, one might cheerfully agree, in the name of intelligence, to let the devil take the hindmost. But the issues have changed since, in the middle of the nineteenth century, the conclusions of positive science clashed with the current religious mythology and won a deserved victory. The clash is now between the inflated mythology of pseudo-science and the very essence of the religious spirit. A cheap Falstaffian realism, without the saving grace of Falstaffian humor, insensible to the finer issues of living and blind to half the evidence of experience, is widely mistaken for a "scientific" frame of mind. Rash and premature speculations as to the ultimate causes of things, and even whole mushroom philosophies based upon hypothetical extensions of scientific laws or supposed laws, have with considerable popular success usurped the place of positive science and claimed the sanction of its name. Child psychology lies about us in our infancy, and various shades of naturalistic philosophy begin to close upon the growing boy. If we were genuinely scientific, these parasitic growths of science would have to face a wholesome skepticism, and we should be continually on our guard, as the true scientist has to be, lest we confuse positive science with hypothetical or philosophical science masquerading in its garments. But we are easily duped, and among the failings of our time I should place first a certain credulousness which, paradoxically enough, takes the form of an outgrowth of our scientific movement.

The second weakness which I wish to stress comes to us as a result of the romantic revolt of the past century and again takes the form of an excess or misapplication of an admirable tendency. Surely there is a time in human affairs for the discarding of outworn institutions, for the opening of the arms to new experience, for the awakening of fresh hopes, and for the challenging of old restraints. Such a moment culminated at the end of the eighteenth century and the beginning of the nineteenth, and we are still acting as its spiritual executors, though signs are not wanting that the estate is nearly settled. We are becoming a little more critical of sentimental experience, a little more doubtful of humanitarian experiment, a little more impatient of unlimited liberty and unchecked individualism than our fathers and grandfathers were. But the great romantic writers, Blake and Wordsworth, Emerson and Thoreau, are still far from outworn. If they offended against the common sense of mankind by revolting against the established agencies of social control, they knew how to make offense a skill by revolting in favor of the severer restraints imposed by their own natures. This willingness of the individual to assume the burden of self-control is the only possible justification of the romantic dream of a better world. In the subsequent enfeebling and debasing of romanticism, however, the principle of inner control has often been lost sight of, and the romantic sentiments of love of absolute unrestraint, universal benevolence, and uncritical tolerance have been substituted for the classical virtues of measure, integrity, and responsibility. In so doing, our feelings have been released from the necessity of finding appropriate expression in action, which the exercise of a virtue involves, and so we have become foolishly drunk upon the dregs of a great vintage.

The effects of romanticism gone stale may be seen in the weak complacency and cynical unconcern with which we too often regard the violation of public trust, the theft of public property, and the endangering of public interests that are precious to us all. We hesitate to set sharp limits to individual freedom of action, even when it damages our own freedom, or to mete out short shrift to an offender, even when we collectively are the injured parties. So the romantic dream of human perfectibility has degenerated into nightmare. And if gold rust what shall iron do? In college communities, where intelligence might be expected, a foolish humanitarian sympathy has all but destroyed the force of conviction necessary to suppress the public nuisance who appropriates to his own use books needed by a group of his fellows or who by dishonorable practices in the classroom destroys the mutual confidence of teacher and student, sullies the reputation of the college, and cheapens the value of its diploma. Surely it is not enough to condemn such offences in a formal constitution, left pretty largely to enforce itself, and to solace offenders with the offer of a helping hand or a second chance to observe the elementary decencies of human intercourse. At any other time but the present an aroused social conscience would quickly find means to make its dictates respected in a region where nature with geological forethought has provided an abundance of stones of a handy size. The easygoing tolerance of antisocial acts is a new thing. It has whatever charm its novelty can bestow, but I hope you will agree with me that that is very little. It is heartening that the past year has brought symptoms of a reviving common sense and communal responsibility in this college. But outside the college you will find the same battle to be fought over again, and the enemy is not so much the reckless individual as it is the apathetic and sentimental majority, willing to condone and reluctant to strike. That feature of our time, I believe, may be counted with its credulousness as a serious weakness.

One possible prophylactic against the excesses or misapplications of the scientific or the romantic spirit consists in becoming a thorough scientist or in perfecting in our own lives the romantic ideal, for in the complete understanding of either science or romanticism there is a saving discipline. But we cannot all be even approximate Emersons or Darwins, and from the danger of such smattering knowledge or imperfect intuition as may fall to our lot the escape lies through great books. I cannot overstress the point that books rightly read have power to mold our characters, to change us for better or for worse, and in this respect reading is the only substitute for the shocks of actual experience. "Who ever heard of anyone being ruined by a book?" asked Mayor James Walker, apropos of the censorship, and did not stay for an answer. If he had read Dante's "Inferno" as far as the fifth canto, he would have heard of two lovers whose passion kindled from the reading of the story of Lancelot and whose undoing followed their unwise choice of a book which only strengthened such impulses as they already possessed too largely by nature. Had they selected Boethius' *On the Consolation of Philosophy*, perchance they might have read further in the book that day, and hell would have lost two of its foremost inhabitants.

Against the flabby sentimentalism and cheap materialism of flatterers and smatterers, if you agree with me that these are prevalent weaknesses of our time, I should suggest the tonic of much reading in the inexhaustible books of our literature, particularly in those that precede the nineteenth century. Let me mention, for illustration and in the hope that one or two of them may become for you an individual possession, a few names, if not of supreme yet of sound writers, such as, in poetry, Donne and Herbert; in prose, the satires of Swift and the novels of Fielding, North's translation of Plutarch and Hoby's version of *The Courtier*, Boswell's *Johnson* and Lockhart's *Life of Scott*, Burke's speeches, and the histories of Prescott and Parkman. The

79

list might be indefinitely extended, but I need not specify such great names as you are all familiar with. Only I should caution you against the common supposition that a single reading of a great author can reveal all that he has to offer. With books as with men friendship is not to be had on easy terms. You must live long with them to pluck the heart out of their mystery. But in so living you may nourish the believing and desiring part of your natures, not with patent medicines compounded of assumed fact, but with the evidence of things not seen which it yet becomes a man to hope for; or you may strengthen yourselves to be positive integers in a plastic world by wrestling with writers of tough intellectual and moral fiber, not letting them go until they have revealed to you your ultimate convictions. Such reading, and the power to master it, should differentiate the college graduate from other men, now as in the past.

Certainly the men whose portraits hang on these walls, and whose names we hold in special reverence because of their long association with this college and their contributions to the cause of learning here, were one and all marked by their devotion to the great books of the ages. And if we could question about our reading in later life one of those sinewy-minded Yankee sages who once filled so sturdily the professorial chairs where we, their punier successors, now rattle, I almost fancy we could hear him answer in his pungent idiom: "Young man, read books that you can have a regular tussle with, books with meat in them that you can set your teeth in, and stay with 'em till you've gnawed the bones and sucked out the marrow—none of your namby-pamby, sugar-coated, sulphur and molasses, young ladies boarding school, lay me out in a hammick in lavender literatoor." Such an instinctive preference for the tried and approved best is our inheritance from the Amherst of the past. When in the course of next year many of you, I hope all of you, find yourselves missing Amherst, when you are homesick for the place, for the friends you have known here, and for the accustomed routine; and when later on you revisit us, only to find another race of undergraduates in your places, unfamiliar buildings crowning College Hill, and even the faculty somewhat altered; then it may console you for the vanishing of what you have known and loved to feel that you may recover all that is essential of Amherst in the pages you have read here. They may be with you always. In what you have found good here, Shakespeare and Milton and others of that glorious company have their part. We hope that you will hold reunions with the spirit of Amherst as you find it in great books, remembering as you read something of this place and believing that as long as the College endures, other boys, such as you once were, will be finding nourishment, though they know it not, from the same pages. May you with Amherst men past and yet to come enter into the joy of that fellowship to which Chaucer's book invites you in the name of all great literature, saying:

> Thorw me men gon into that blysful place
> Of hertis hele, and dedly woundis cure;
> Thorw me men gon onto the welle of grace,
> There grene and lusty May shal evere endure;
> This is the weye to al good aventure.
> Be glad, thow redere, and thy sorwe ofcaste,
> Al opyn am I, passe in, and sped the faste.

The Soul of a College [1]

SOME ninety years ago, Emerson—perhaps feeling as flattered and as flustered as I do now—opened his address to the graduating class at the Divinity School, Cambridge, by recalling to his hearers the loveliness of New England landscape.

In this refulgent summer, it has been a luxury to draw the breath of life. The grass grows, the buds burst, the meadow is spotted with fire and gold in the tint of flowers. . . . Night brings no gloom to the heart with its welcome shade. Through the transparent darkness the stars pour their almost spiritual rays.

The same luxury of translucent blue afternoons that one might wish would never end has been yours at intervals during this spring of your senior year. I trust that you have found in the suavity and graciousness of these last Amherst

[1] An address given at the Senior Chapel exercises of the Class of 1930.

days a partial offset for the impressions left with you by the late winter of our discontent.

Not in every place, nor always here in our capricious climate, does the charm of our surroundings afford a recompense for man's alleged inhumanity to man. But the need of finding compensations for the inevitable disappointments and afflictions of life is universal, and it is a sign of wisdom to find them habitually in the little satisfactions of our daily routine, in the joys of food and sleep and exercise and the conversation of friends. This point is beautifully illustrated in a story by Willa Cather telling of a Nebraska farmer who, when his corn was roasted in the field by a scorching sun, immediately took the occasion to make holiday with his family. Rather than submit to the bitterness of despair in the loss of his crops, he chose to enjoy fried chicken and coffee, the cool of twilight and children's laughter. In case you should ever again encounter such stringencies as you have complained of during the past year, I commend to you the example of this unlettered farmer—with the secret conviction that about one good afternoon and a very little fried chicken will prove a sufficient poultice for such wounds.

The American undergraduate, in general, is sometimes suspected of failing to appreciate his opportunities. He is supposed to approach the gates of his Alma Mater in the nonchalant fashion of the cat described by an Amherst writer:

> The door is opened at his mew,
> And then you have to push him through.

I do not imagine that any such suspicion is justified here. I believe rather that Amherst students and teachers have always felt a community of interest deeper than any super-

ficial misunderstandings can disturb. But because the occasional acerbities of our official relationship naturally attract
more attention than the continuing norm of our mutual
regard, I should like to devote these last words that I have
the honor of speaking to you to a consideration of what it is
that holds the members of a college together, in spite of the
proverbial and potential and sometimes actual divergencies
between crabbéd age and crabbing youth.

Is there any cohesive force, any principle of integration
that gives form to an institution, as the soul in scholastic
philosophy was supposed to give form and organization to
the body? I have cast the question deliberately in old-
fashioned terms, using the discredited word "soul," because
we are about to examine a kind of experience which is not
precisely measurable and which, therefore, may be more
easily described in poetic than in scientific language. I
hope, however, that the comparison of a college to a human personality will be intelligible even to those who have
been brought up to think that man is a system of electrons
rather than that man is a soul. Without a soul, according to
St. Thomas Aquinas, man would be merely a heap of jar-
ring atoms, or if you like, electrons on the loose without
a system. He or it might well be described, in the ungallant
phrase recently employed by one of our undergraduate
writers in picturing one of the fairer sex, as "only a piece
of sweaty meat." Between man so conceived and man in
full possession of his human faculties, integrated by the
union of soul with body, the difference is enormous and
readily perceptible. Can we recognize the same difference
between a factory and a college, between institutions that
men live by and institutions that men live for? And if so,
wherein does the soul of a college lie?

Poetry and Civilization

It does not lie, I think, in our ordinary business of giving and receiving instruction. The same thing may be and is done by night schools and correspondence courses in a perfectly material and soulless way. The college may put its soul into teaching, but it is not from the classroom that it gets its soul. Sharpening the mind of youth on the whetstone of irregular verbs or their equivalent is not its life, but its usual means of livelihood, its bread and butter. Therefore if any faculty of the soul is involved in teaching, it is only the lowest of the three faculties, which Aristotle called the vegetative, meaning that which causes nourishment and growth in a physical sense. "This faculty," he remarks further, "is thought to work most in time of sleep"—an observation which tends to confirm my analysis. In so far as the college is a machine for turning out trained minds, it is comparable to a factory and is paid for its product as a factory is paid. There is nothing spiritual in the transaction.

It would be tempting, on the other hand, to suppose that the soul of a college resides in that blend of exuberance and loyalty called college spirit. The cult of Alma Mater has indeed become almost a religion with us. It has its high priests, not to mention its whirling dervishes, among both undergraduate and alumni bodies. But though it is intensely bound up with our conception of a college, it is not, I believe, what essentially unites the college, for the urges of college spirit have been known to run counter to the deeper purposes of the institution. So I should prefer to associate it with the second inferior faculty of the soul, again according to Aristotle, the sensitive or animal part of the soul, which is capable of being guided, though at times it fights and strains against reason. College spirit is a reservoir of energy and vigor, but it does not rule and guide.

The Soul of a College

We may simplify our search for the integrating principle of a college if we strip the institution to its essence, and conceive it for a moment, not as it commonly exists in imperfect mixture with worldly necessities, but in pure form comparable to Plato's ideal city in the sky. Yet to avoid too prolonged an excursion into the inane, let me choose for illustration a college which approximates the ideal, in the Platonic sense, and which actually exists.

There is, I am told, in Oxford a certain college that has no undergraduates, and consequently no alumni and no teaching faculty. It used to maintain in residence four undergraduate scholars, or "Bible clerks" as they were called; but it so happened at one time that all four incumbents were enthusiastic oarsmen, and so they put a boat on the river and raced four-oared crews from other colleges and actually won the championship in their class. Thereupon the faculty, fearing perhaps that the animal part of the soul was about to dominate the rational, abolished the student body once for all. Since then the college has gone serenely on its way, a warden and fifty fellows engaged in learning for learning's sake. Men do not graduate from this college. They spend their lives there.

At times, I confess, I cannot help thinking of this college as very nearly ideal. But I do not mean that I should like to see it widely imitated, and I trust none of you will ever highly resolve to endow anything of the kind. That would be a pathetic blunder. It is not important that ideal things should exist in fact; it is only important that they should be kept in mind so that men may take their bearings by them and not get lost amid the confusions and pretenses of the actual world. So I cite the example of the ideal college, which may as well be in the sky as in Oxford, to enforce the point that a college is in essence a community of men of any age dedicated to the enterprise of learning. By its devotion to learning a college is integrated and given form. It achieves a corporate soul.

This conclusion, I am aware, may sound to many of you as fantastic as the process by which it has been reached. Everybody knows that our colleges turn out as many bond salesmen as disciples of learning. I am coming to that point later. Meanwhile some may object that in speaking of the corporate soul of a college I am using a meaningless metaphor, that in plain language an institution has no soul. I must insist, however, that the poetic analogy here employed is as precisely descriptive of fact as some formulas that even the most scrupulous and literal-minded people accept without hesitation. For example, we are resorting to a figment of the imagination when we speak of the magnetic pole. No one has ever seen it or had it in his pocket. We see the action of compass needles, and we attribute their behavior to an unseen force and give it a name and local habitation. Similarly, if we discern the presence of an organizing and shaping force in the actions of men, a kind of polarizing power that overcomes their habitual inertia, we are not being unduly fanciful if we describe this power by a collective term, such as a corporate soul. What is important, however, is not the label we affix, but the reality for which the label stands. Let us then look behind the words into the stuff of experience itself, taking our examples from the history of the institution that we know most intimately.

If from our distance in time we look back on this Hampshire County region one hundred and ten years ago, as though we were watching the actions of ants about an anthill, we can hardly fail to notice signs of an unusual and curious excitement. People were doing things that could not be explained by any of the ordinary human desires for comfort, prosperity, or pleasure. Their lives were being swept into a common pattern as though they were iron filings brought within the field of a powerful magnet. Men were giving their money and bequeathing their property, not to their families, not to any object from which they hoped for material reward, but to establish a fund for classical and Christian education, to found a charitable institution, to erect a college building or chapel. Two citizens in particular, one the leading lawyer of this village, gave so freely of their time and substance that they impoverished themselves. And they were but the leaders of an uncounted number, including women and children, who out of needy nothing gave more than they could spare in order that an institution dedicated entirely to things of the spiritual order might flourish among them. The people of the region, as we say poetically and accurately, put their souls into the work, and what they put in was put to stay.

Twenty-five years later we may again discern the same inexplicable force at work, holding the College together in time of distress. The day of small local enterprises was passing. Amherst Academy could not survive the movement for popular and practical education that was sweeping the country. It was obvious that the College likewise could no longer be maintained by local resources, there were no benefactors in sight, and it seemed to many friends of the institution that the enterprise would have to be abandoned. Then an incalculable thing happened. The president of Amherst, a distinguished scientist, and his faculty, all of them able clergymen, announced that if the College could not pay them their salaries, they would stay for whatever the College could afford to pay. They did so, and for some years received a pittance that would not hire a laboratory assistant nowadays. Then little by little help came. But I ask you to think of what those lean years meant. It would have been easy for that band of nine professors, particularly easy for their president, to find an adequate livelihood elsewhere, to advance themselves professionally, to benefit their families. But turn to our "Biographical Record" and you will see that not a single professor resigned between 1845 and 1850, except one who left in broken health and a few months later "passed out of record into renown."

To understand the spirit that informed the men who stood by the College in its dark hour, let us abandon the long perspective of years and come as close as we may to one of them. I am not selecting any of the notable names of Amherst history, but a somewhat obscure professor, who taught here for only six years, being appointed at his own request in 1847 to the chair of astronomy and zoology. This man, who was a graduate of our college in the class of 1834, had been a professor at Middlebury College and state geologist of Vermont. He had already given promise of distinguished achievement as a scientist when he elected to throw in his lot with an ill-endowed college at the very moment when its continued existence seemed most precarious. Though he had studied many branches of science, his main interest was in zoology, and for collecting and classifying shellfish he had a veritable passion. By sheer persistence, for he never had any money to spare, he had amassed a collection of shells from all parts of the world, valued when he came here at fully five times the amount of his annual salary. Almost his first act was to present this collection to the College in order that its prestige as a scientific institution.might be increased. Amherst College might be about to fail, but at least it would go down with the best collection of shells in the United States. So he spent his days and nights cataloguing and improving his collection. In the sympathetic words of President Hitchcock, "So economical was he of his time, that in going from his cabinet to his meals he had learnt to move upon a trot, and I am afraid that too many midnight hours saw his lamp burning." He worked on till he had brought together some eight thousand specimens and had, in the opinion of Louis Agassiz, the most remarkable collection of its kind in the whole country. Then still in pursuit of shellfish, he visited the West Indies, contracted yellow fever, and died at the age of thirty-six, a martyr to molluscs. Not long ago a Williams senior touring the Virgin Islands found his forgotten tombstone and wrote to tell us that "a warm sun passes over, and friendly little green lizards dart across the grave of an Amherst man who did his work well and generously."

No doubt this professor with his mania for collecting imagined that he was doing something important and necessary in cataloguing his specimens. That, of course, was his pet delusion. We hardly know now what to do with the shells he has bequeathed us, and over his scientific papers time has mercifully passed an expunging hand. From a detached standpoint his absorption in shellfish seems as quaint as most things that professors get excited about. That, however, is hardly the point. There was published recently the narrative of a seafaring man who in the course of duty was assigned the task of steering a lifeboat to a steamer foundering in a gale, picking its crew out of the tumultuous waters, and taking his loaded boat back again to his own vessel. He accomplished the feat, and this was what the experience of being the hero of that rescue meant to him. "In later years he whispered to himself that, for one moment or one hour of his life, he was able to forget himself. And for that he was forever thankful." [2] If a blunt, practical seaman may think himself fortunate to be caught up for a single hour and merged in the soul of an enterprise, may we not consider our professor trotting back to his cabinet day after day with his mind so intent on his beloved labors that he had no time to wonder where his next meal was coming from, and indeed could hardly spare the time to eat at all—may we not think of him as one of the most blest of men? But for him and his colleagues, so devoted to the subjects of their study that their personal fortunes did not seem much to matter, Amherst College might have looked long and in vain for rescue.

There is not time to extend the litany of our heroes further, nor is there need in this company to bring the list within the range of present memory. I have chosen my illustrations from men long out of mind, not even mentioning names, since my purpose is less to celebrate individuals, however worthy of honor, than to exemplify the power of integration and dedication that breathed upon them and made them its living instruments. We have a song called "The Soul of Old Amherst," which we hear sung annually at the Commencement exercises, but we seldom speak with conviction of the conception underlying the words or attribute to them any but a sentimental meaning. Of course our spiritual heirlooms are not for display in the front windows, but it would be an equal mistake to leave them perpetually undusted. They deserve to be bur-

[2] Captain George H. Grant, "The Rescue," *Atlantic Monthly* (April 1930).

nished by meditation and kept shining in whatever closet
of the heart we reserve for things most precious. For the
community of men that does not feel itself animated and
lifted by an influence greater than the sum of the individual forces composing it is poor indeed. Without a sense
of commitment to an enterprise of larger scope than the
task of training boys, a college may easily degenerate. It may
gently lapse into a coterie of country gentlemen, content
to entertain the harmless day with a familiar book or golf,
or it may split into warring cabals of petty politicians, concerned to regulate each other's conduct by barbershop tac-
tics and spreading jealousy and dislike like barber's itch.
It shall not degenerate, however, while it remains mindful
of the effluence transmitted from the earnest men who gave
themselves unstintedly that the College might have being
and prosper, while the ranks of its faculty are filled by its
own graduates and by those others indistinguishable from
them who are poets, historians, philosophers, artists, and
scientists by vocation and teachers by fortunate accident,
and while its attention is steadily focused outward, beyond
the daily routine of recitation and examination, upon the
old and endlessly hopeful enterprise of learning. Such a
college may indeed lift up men's hearts. It has kept faith
with its soul.

I have been speaking hitherto of the essential meaning
of a college in its inward working, chiefly as reflected in the
lives of those who feel its influence most intensely. But
I have not forgotten the bond salesmen—using the word,
not as a term of reproach, but simply to designate by
metonymy that irreclaimable minimum of our students who,
though not impervious to learning, yet after four years gasp-
ing in collegiate air plunge with relief into the roily waters

of utilitarian pursuits. What does the soul of a college mean to these useful citizens?

They tend, of course, to demand that the college be serviceable to them and to look for no further significance than the practical advantages accruing from a college training. But if we try to justify a college in terms of its usefulness, how pathetically we miss its finer essence, how much remains unexplained! A contemporary of mine once told me that the only bright spot in his course in freshman mathematics was the moment when the class came to an algebraic formula for calculating compound interest. Here at last was a plain and palpable labor-saving device. My friend seized upon it and made it his own. Then, after college, he became a minister of the gospel. Needless to say, he has never had any occasion to use the formula for calculating compound interest and his knowledge of it has long since atrophied for want of exercise.

While looking for the useful and practical my friend missed a beauty that Euclid alone has looked upon unveiled but that even the humblest of his followers may glimpse in part. In his *Poetry and Mathematics* Mr. Scott Buchanan says:

The structures with which mathematics deals are more like lace, the leaves of trees, and the play of light and shadow on a meadow or a human face, than they are like buildings and machines, the least of their representatives. The best proofs in mathematics are short and crisp like epigrams, and the longest have swings and rhythms that are like music. The structures of mathematics and the propositions about them are ways for the imagination to travel and the wings, or legs, or vehicles to take you where you want to go . . . on the journey fantastic.

The Soul of a College

These are the words of a devotee, for whom abstract relationships move in a kind of glory. They may preserve us, who look askance on algebra, from resting satisfied with the practical advantages of a college education.

What else has a college, an institution that deals in what is not bread alone, to offer to practical people? I think this: the example of a disinterested life, which may be practiced here and remembered and continued later. You cannot touch learning without becoming impersonal. You cannot pursue it very far without gaining a vantage ground of detachment. And the further you go the more habitually you come to consider your individual concerns and private feelings as though they were figures in a morality play enacted for your entertainment, where you may see Pride wounded and Vanity made ridiculous and even True-Love scorned, knowing these puppets for your own, and yet realizing that the action of their tragi-comic interlude is not of supreme importance. So much you may have gathered from your sojourn here.

You have shared for a time in the activities of a college and are now to follow the very diverse occupations of the world, some perhaps to preach bonds, others to peddle philosophy or literature. You will discover soon, I hope, that you have a bond of union in what you have comprehended and made your own of the spirit of the College, that in becoming a part of Amherst you have also become an integer of soul.

Education for Democracy [1]

GENTLEMEN of the Class of 1945—who like Shakespeare's Macduff are from your Alma Mater's womb untimely ripp'd: I have no intention of laying upon your twenty-eight shoulders today the burdens under which our civilization labors. The time is past when with every recurring June Commencement speakers could call upon a new crop of college graduates to go forth and save the world. Our common salvation is an enterprise in which every man, woman, and child must share to the extent of his capacity. Each of you, if you have not already

[1] Excerpts from an address given at the Senior Chapel exercises of the Class of 1945. The class of 1945, because of the accelerated program of the war years, graduated in 1944.

For the past five years Amherst College has had "one-hundred-per-cent rushing"; every freshman has been invited to join one of the social groups. In the long campaign that preceded this achievement Professor Whicher's speech was of first importance.

97

found your place, will shortly find it. But before you leave this spot, where you have been all but completely sheltered from the stresses of our era, it is not unfitting that we should consider together whether your college can do anything to sustain the cause in which we are all engaged. And in speaking on this theme I am addressing not merely you who hear my voice, but your former classmates who are no longer here and all our younger alumni on whom the destinies of Amherst will rest in the years immediately ahead.

You will understand that I am speaking as an individual member of the Amherst community, and at a time when the fullest expression of opinion on the part of individuals seems desirable.

Very nearly a century and a quarter ago this college was founded with a bold and ambitious program; its avowed object was "to civilize and evangelize the world by the classical education of indigent young men of piety and talents." One is tempted to exclaim that never have so few undertaken to do so much for so many—or with more pathetically inadequate means. Nevertheless a college dedicated to such an objective was not likely to lose the name of action, and what Amherst missionaries accomplished in Syria and Turkey, in Hawaii and China, was not inconsiderable. Ralph Waldo Emerson, inspecting Amherst while the first fervor of its dedication was still upon it, described the institution as "an infant Hercules."

It was not often that Emerson gave his approval to anything academic. Hardly fifteen years after his Amherst visit he pronounced in his famous Phi Beta Kappa address a withering indictment of the American intellectual. Our thinkers, he held, were derivative and timid. "The scholar is decent, indolent, complaisant." This indictment still stands.

98

It applies with double force to organizations of scholars. For an example it is only necessary to read a little further in the history of this college.

In 1833, during the first access of antislavery agitation in the North, the students of Amherst formed both a Colonization Society to promote the mitigation of slavery by gentle measures and an Anti-Slavery Society to campaign for its immediate abolition. Debate waxed fierce. There were here at that time an unusual number of students from the southern states. The College was soon divided into two bitterly contending camps. Then, as Professor Tyler tells it in his *History of Amherst College:*

The Faculty seeing that fellow-students, and even Christian brethren were thus set in hostile array against each other, feeling that the College was not founded to be a school of moral or political reform, and fearing that its reputation, as well as its peace and prosperity might thus be endangered, at length interposed, and endeavored to persuade the members of both societies to dissolve their organizations.

When the members of the Anti-Slavery Society refused on high grounds of conscience to comply, the faculty at length proceeded to suppress the society by fiat.

Tyler traces to this action, even though it was rescinded a few years later, the first rift in the previously cordial relations between Amherst students and faculty. The College in its corporate capacity had lagged behind the moral sense of its most high-minded constituents. In the years that followed, Amherst graduates contributed to the fight against slavery, though the most effective blow of all was struck by a woman, the sister of an Amherst alumnus. The College officially guarded its peace, increased its material prosperity,

99

and left it to Harriet Beecher Stowe to win reputation by standing up for her convictions.

As a further commentary I should like to cite the actions of two organized religious bodies on this same question of Negro slavery. The Quakers under the promptings of John Woolman and others took very early cognizance of the problem. Long before slavery had become a "peculiar institution" that men would die to defend, they considered it in the quietness of thought, condemned it on principle, and eradicated slaveholding among the members of their communion. In consequence of having taken positive moral action they were unshaken when the country divided on the issue. In contrast to the Quakers, the Methodists, certainly no less godly as individuals, delayed in making up their minds, postponed the issue, and found it inexpedient to do anything decisive. Eventually they were caught in the division of the country and rent apart with it.

The moral for institutional bodies would seem to be this: avoidance of political action is itself a form of political action. It differs from other forms of action only in being negative and generally ineffective. The old ostrich dodge is a close cousin to the discredited policy of appeasement, of which we have seen enough to last us for several generations.

As long as the nineteenth-century current of liberalism retained its force, it was possible for American colleges to stand aloof from political questions. No basic changes in the structure of human society were involved. Whatever side won, the fundamental value of humanity remained secure. Now, however, the possibility of such aloofness is rapidly diminishing. It seems not unlikely that in the postwar era this college and other institutions that cherish a liberal tradition cannot afford to take an indifferent attitude to the social and political changes that affect the society in which we have our being. They must either become schools of moral and political reform, or they must acquiesce in a growing contempt for things of the mind and sink to the level of mere nurseries where young Americans congregate to pass through an unthinking larval stage as complaisantly as caterpillars. Certain political tendencies are now abroad which if they become dominant involve the extinction of every value for which the liberal college stands. They are not the peculiar property of German Nazis or Japanese imperialists; the seeds of fascism exist in every human heart. So it is not impossible that the Fascist system, if checked in Europe, will next manifest itself in some equivalent form in the Western Hemisphere.

In saying this I am not thinking of the Argentine and Bolivia. I would not presume to speak of South American affairs. But I am concerned for what may happen here in our midst. Let us in all humility keep in mind that we have seen a pretty good imitation Mussolini capture the political machinery of one of our states and become in effect its dictator; and in his rise to power Huey Long, the Duce of Louisiana, did not encounter much opposition from people devoted to democratic institutions. What stopped him was an assassin's bullet. Have we anything better than that to trust to when the next political gangster sees the United States as an easy mark and sets out to make himself its overlord?

. . . . .

What is to be the attitude of the College, and, more important, what forms of action can it take? It can, and does, offer a course for freshmen in problems of democracy. Were it a matter of promoting an understanding of a foreign culture the offering of a course might be a helpful and even a sufficient gesture. But we are now concerned not simply with comprehension but with patterns of behavior. Since courses must be given with academic impartiality, the curriculum is not a place for propaganda or proselyting, even in the best of causes. Theoretically a student might complete the course as a convinced democrat with a better understanding of the methods of fascism, or as a convinced Fascist with a further contempt for the weaknesses of democracy. In any case I do not believe that giving a course on a critical political issue is a sufficient response for a college to make. Its reaction must go deeper than the curriculum; its concern must be a matter of twenty-four hours a day, not merely of three hours a week. The whole life and structure of the college community should give expression to its vital convictions. If we believe in the inviolable dignity of the individual, if we prefer democratic procedures, if we have faith in intelligence and reasonableness, if we think it important that actions should correspond to professions, then it is not too much to ask that these convictions should be visibly manifested in our institutional forms and daily customs.

I suppose the function of a liberal college as it has developed in America does not reside chiefly in the disciplines of the classroom. If it did we should feel bound to see that they were better enforced than they generally are at present. I suppose that the real value of a college experience is that it confirms the participant in a way of life characterized in the main by fairness, good sportsmanship, and a regard for humane considerations, and implants this so deeply that nothing which may happen later in life can quite shake it out of him. For this reason a three-year college course, though it contrive to cover as many hours in class, can never have the same effect as a four-year course. If this is so, then it becomes a vital concern to the college and to the society it serves to see that the way of life it inculcates fully bears out the humanity it professes.

The lesson most painfully impressed upon us by the breakdown of civilization in our generation is that free institutions cannot be established once for all and then left to take care of themselves. They have to be continuously maintained. There is no liberty, as Milton insisted, except "strenuous liberty." This means that the Fascist tendencies that lie latent among us must be stopped before they can get started. Like the grasshopper plagues on the middle west frontier, a Fascist outbreak may become uncontrollable if it is allowed to gather impetus; the only way to control it is to discover and eradicate its breeding places. Then the swarming and the senseless fury of destruction cannot occur.

One fertile breeding ground of fascism is found notoriously in racial hatreds and religious intolerance. Whenever one group of men, whether clique, cult, caste, class, or race, feeds on the delusion of its superiority to other groups or races, it is easy for a dictator to sway them by appeals to both pride and fear, for every social injustice brings with it an unconscious dread of retribution. Our ordinary approach to such situations is, I think, often less effective than it might be, because we have acquired a humanitarian habit of sympathizing with the wrongs of oppressed minorities, and sympathy like other emotional reactions can be exhausted by continual use. The insensate cruelties and bestialities inspired by the myth of Aryan dominance have so seared our sensibilities that they can hardly respond any more even to the most hideous enormities. A more profitable approach is to study as sociologists the causes that produce outbreaks of aggressive superiority and to consider as moralists the deterioration that ensues in the character of the supposed master race. The daily papers provide much laboratory material, not always confined to Germany and Japan. Mr. E. M. Forster's unforgettable novel, *A Passage to India*, presents a fully detailed case history, revealing the uneasy hatreds, suspicions, violences, and jealousies, the products of an ever-present substratum of fear, that have afflicted the British ruling class in India. The recent race riots in Detroit may remind us that even here in the United States we cannot claim exemption from the doom that clings like a shadow to any assertion of a fictitious superiority.

American colleges have been notably democratic. They have been much less associated with the idea of a privileged class than their English prototypes, Oxford and Cambridge, have been. Amherst is bound by the terms of its charter to make no distinction among its students because of religious creed. The College has welcomed from its earliest days men from foreign lands and men of every race and color. One of the very first Negroes to graduate from any American college or university graduated from Amherst in 1826. Among our distinguished living graduates are Chinese, Armenians, and orthodox Hebrews. The portrait of a Japanese educator holds a place of honor in our Chapel. These are items in our record that we may justly be proud of and seek to multiply.

At the present time the College is preparing to receive delegations of students from a number of the allied nations, to be educated here at the expense of their governments. This is not only an opportunity to render an appropriate service to countries where education has been disrupted by the war. It is also an opportunity for our students to learn much from the politically more mature students from abroad.

Beyond receiving refugee students the College can do little under wartime conditions. But immediately after the war it might well take measures to see that our tradition of racial tolerance is consciously maintained. The relation between whites and Negroes is one of the most delicate problems that this country has to handle. If it is shirked by educated men, it will be handled by the uneducated in a way that is not pretty to contemplate. For the good of us all, therefore, there ought to be a fair number of Negroes in every class that enters Amherst. While anti-Semitism is rampant in the world and signs of the infection are not wanting in this country, is it not incumbent on us to do more than we have ever done for the education of boys of Jewish ancestry? When this vilest of outlandish frenzies threatens to corrupt and undo our civilization, the part of sane and responsible men is not to stand virtuously apart but to counteract it.

Furthermore every boy who enters Amherst College should be entitled to share in all the privileges that the college community offers. In spite of the palliation provided by the Lord Jeff Club, this has not been true in recent years. Officially the College welcomes all students on the same terms. Unofficially the college community says in effect to the young men who enter Amherst: "Nine out of every ten of you will be admitted to all the privileges of our common life. One will be denied the important privilege of membership in our student societies. If he is a Negro, there is absolutely no chance of his being taken into the fellowship of a fraternity; if he is a Jew the chances are against his being invited; if he is a Chinese, paradoxically, the chances are pretty good of his making a fraternity. And if, being Aryan, he conspicuously lacks the social graces that association with fraternity mates is supposed to bestow, he will probably be rejected." It is a historical accident that this kind of discrimination has come into existence here. No one deliberately planned it so. But that is no reason why the system should not be modified to suit the exigencies of changing times.

Originally our fraternities were organized as selective bodies, little groups of students who banded together in the intensity of their interest in the intellectual work of the College. Modern fraternity groups have totally lost this pristine character. They are nothing but social groups. As such they have an opportunity to become a functional part of the College by reversing their traditional policy of exclusiveness and assuming responsibility for the social life of the entire student body. If they refuse all functional activity and remain an impediment in the life of the College, I cannot see how they can long avoid the fate of the sterile and the outworn.

I submit that if Amherst means to be a democratic college and to train men for citizenship in a democratic society, it cannot lightly brush aside a situation so incongruous with its aims with the remark that of course the fraternities are undemocratic, but—. There is only one rule for a vigorous community of equals and that is embodied in Whitman's words: "By God! I will accept nothing which all cannot have their counterpart of on the same terms." I am not thinking of the effect of exclusiveness on the men left out so much as on the men who join the fraternities and suffer the insidious vanity of believing themselves among the specially privileged. What kind of flattering unction are we encouraging these youngsters to lay to their souls? Does the fact of their member-

ship in an exclusive group delude them into a complacent
attitude toward their appalling mediocrity? That is what the
illusion of superiority often does. There is snobbishness
enough spontaneously generated in human intercourse without letting it get entrenched in our system of training youth.

· · · · ·

I have suggested that the College assume a militant attitude toward the problems of racial intolerance and international misunderstanding rather than let the conditions
under which a college can exist at all go by default. There
is one more pressing duty that confronts the faculties of
American institutions of learning in general: to see to it
that the machinery of education is not captured by and
used to further the interests of any entrenched reactionary
groups in our economy. All our colleges, and this college
in particular, owe a great debt of appreciation to the busi-
nessmen who with genuinely enlightened ideals of education and with unstinted devotion have labored to extend
and improve American higher education. But the dominance
of what may be called management in education is every-
where increasing. It is not good for college professors, or for
any other class of independent workers, to be too much
controlled, even for their own benefit. The men who teach
must control the business of education just as much as
doctors must control the operation of a hospital. Any other
arrangement leads to the deterioration of responsibility on
the part of the faculty and opens the way for ultimate ex-
ploitation. Here at Amherst, where the relations of trustees
and faculty have been ideally sympathetic, the question
of the role of the faculty in determining the policies of the
institution might well be re-examined and reformulated

with the aim of establishing a model for the rest of the country.

In the postwar world college faculties might well take a more active part than they have hitherto taken in placing our young graduates where their training will be of greatest benefit to our country. Between the British universities and the Civil Service there exists an unofficial but helpful liaison: the moment a vacancy occurs in any of the services the head of some Oxford or Cambridge college starts moving heaven and earth to get one of his graduates appointed to the post. In this country the business of our government promises to become one of the most important spheres of action that a young man can enter. It ought to attract an increasing proportion of our most able college men. Who could ask for a more richly satisfying career than that of our late trustee, Joseph B. Eastman, appointed to the Interstate Commerce Commission by a succession of presidents who could not afford to dispense with his services, and ultimately acknowledged as the supreme public authority in all matters of transportation? What greater service could a college man render than to supply an element of stability, courage, and vision to the direction of national affairs? This country cannot be run without a highly trained, professional corps of experts, comparable to the British Civil Service. Men for this purpose must be recruited largely from the colleges. Might not Amherst, with its fine tradition of public service, be a deliberate pioneer in placing men of the highest caliber in government, not as politicians but as public servants? Can we indeed afford to let our best men go into commerce and industry while there is crying need for trained intelligence in the administration of our increasingly complex democracy?

Education for Democracy

If this college and others like it do not make their convictions felt in some such ways as these, they will have only themselves to blame if the public loses respect for education and educators. No one respects the impotent. It was a little group of determined American provincials—fewer in number than the Amherst faculty—who signed a document reading in part: "We hold these truths to be self-evident. . . . And for the support of this declaration . . . we mutually pledge to each other our lives, our fortunes, and our sacred honor." It is as clear now as it was then that no one is going to save our freedom for us if we do not save it for ourselves. Let us declare in no uncertain terms, "We hold these truths to be self-evident," and we intend to keep on holding them and applying them to as large a segment of the world as we can control, no matter what theme song is being sounded from the international band wagon.

The Arts

in the College Curriculum [1]

AFTER many wanderings the faculty of Amherst College has returned to hold its meetings in the Octagon at the exact spot where the College was born. Over a century ago the old village meetinghouse, which occupied the site of this building, was the scene of earnest debates concerning the foundation of a new institution and its proper location in western Massachusetts; furthermore, it was the place where, on September 18, 1821, Zephaniah Swift Moore was inaugurated as the first president of the College, and where the Amherst faculty was brought into being by the installation of a single professor.

[1] This address was delivered at the dedication of the Frank L. Babbott Faculty Room on May 3, 1935. Since that date Professor Whicher's hope that students might find more opportunity, within the academic curriculum, for the practice of the arts, has been amply fulfilled.

Poetry and Civilization

Other memories woven into the spiritual texture of Amherst College are connected with the building in which we are gathered. Late in June 1848 the Woods Cabinet and Lawrence Observatory, then newly erected where the meetinghouse had stood, was the center of interest at the dedication ceremonies which marked the renaissance of this college after its almost fatal decline at the end of President Humphrey's administration. On that occasion the trustees invited all the benefactors of the institution to be present for a general celebration to see the gratifying changes that their liberality had made possible. President Hitchcock proudly called the attention of his honored guests to the window blinds recently placed on the dormitories, mentioned with expressions of gratitude the several professorships endowed, and as a climax pointed to the new cabinet and the rich collections it contained. This building was in fact the visible sign that Amherst College had emerged from an era of depression and was looking with hope and energy to an assured future.

As the first building erected for a particular purpose, the Woods Cabinet was likewise a sign that science had firmly entrenched itself in the Amherst curriculum. The change symbolized in the transition from meetinghouse to museum was not lost on some of the distinguished visitors who, in the interval between the formal exercises and dinner, were given an opportunity to inspect the geological and zoological collections now first opened to the public. While gazing on the newly acquired Shepard minerals which filled the cases in this room, on the fossil footprints which President Hitchcock was then inclined to attribute to a gigantic bird of ostrich kind, on the Adams collection of shells and insects, and on hundreds of other specimens gathered by devoted professors and missionaries from all parts of the world, the more pious spectators became uneasily conscious that the College was devoting a good deal of attention to an interest not strictly consonant with the religious aims of its founders. It was all very well for Professor Adams to explain that the purpose of these collections was to exhibit "the glorious plan of creation . . . as this exists in the Divine Mind," but where among these rocks and molluscs and bird tracks was the needful evidence of the still more important plan of man's salvation? Man, indeed, was not forgotten. In the words of President Hitchcock's catalogue, he was "deservedly placed at the head of the Class Mammalia"; and in the case devoted to the human form were displayed an articulated skeleton, a manikin which could be taken apart to show all the organs of the body in their proper places, size, and color, and two enlarged models of the human eye and ear. "In the same case," the catalogue continued with unconscious humor, "is exhibited a fine specimen of a double calf presented by Dr. Anthony Jones of Newburyport." In this context it was difficult to recall that man was made a little lower than the angels. The remarks of several speakers at the dinner were obscurely troubled by such considerations. Governor Armstrong, for example, in congratulating the College on the "beautiful structure" so admirably designed to increase the students' acquaintance with the stars, hoped that while they looked upon those beautiful orbs of the sky, they would never forget the Star of Bethlehem. President Hitchcock and his faculty, however, felt no misgivings, and to them the construction of the Octagon meant the coming of a brighter day to Amherst College.

About 1908 the geological collections were moved to new

quarters and the Octagon was assigned to the Department of Music. It thus became the first building on the campus given over to the teaching of one of the arts. As far as I can discover this event was never properly solemnized and our Music Department remains to this day unconsecrated. But long before it became the seat of musical instruction, this building had, without anyone's intending it, brought the subject of artistic taste prominently into notice. Its unique plan, for which President Hitchcock was primarily responsible, raised for the first time in Amherst an aesthetic problem. Its sponsor tells us in his *Reminiscences of Amherst College*:

When it was finished, some of our good friends who had never seen the architecture of Europe, were greatly scandalized because the building had so many angles, and its longer axis or front was not perpendicular to the face of the buildings behind, but quite oblique, conforming to the crest of the hill. But gentlemen who have studied the architecture of Europe, and the effect of form and position, have again and again expressed to me their admiration of this building in connection with its surroundings. Nor will future additions to this pile detract from its harmony and beauty, if made by a skillful architect. This is the first building on the College Hill that showed anything like architectural symmetry and effect, except the President's house. It is no wonder that it should greatly disturb the ideas of a man whose highest notion of architectural beauty is a right angle and a parallelopiped.

But in spite of President Hitchcock's hearty defense the Octagon has remained to this day a disturber of aesthetic peace. Perhaps the nadir of appreciation was reached when Professor Genung led a friend from Williams past it, endeavoring by animated conversation to distract his attention, only to be interrupted by the query, "Is that your gashouse?" This was the comment of an alien spirit. "Nungie" was more discerning than his friend when he wrote subsequently: "A great deal of the sturdy old Amherst gleams forth from that odd piece of architecture; it stands there not for idle and unsympathetic tourists to see, but for alumni to cherish and remember." This opinion may be confirmed if we study President Hitchcock's instructions to his architect, which, if we discount his eccentric fondness for eight-sided buildings, are a model of what such instructions should be:

I said to him, I want you should make both the Cabinet and Observatory octagonal, and of such dimensions as you can with the money we have on hand, taking care not to leave us a cent in debt. Adapt the building to the shape, size, and position of the hill, and give it such a form that other buildings can be added to it hereafter without marring the plan.

It is not too fanciful to believe that something of the homely idiom and transparent honesty of these instructions were reflected in the architect's design.

The company that assembled to celebrate the dedication of the Octagon eighty-seven years ago would, however, have been perplexed by the idea that a college building was to be judged by any standards other than those of utility. Among the distinguished visitors was the elder Professor Silliman of Yale, the instructor of both President Hitchcock and Professor Shepard, and a notable pioneer in the teaching of science. In the history of American aesthetics, too, Professor Silliman has a place, since his remarks to a Yale freshman who dared to introduce wallpaper and a carpet into his college room may be taken as indicative of the absolute bedrock on which all that we mean by an aesthetic sense had still to be erected. "All this love of externals, young man," the professor thundered, "argues indifference to the more necessary furniture of the brain, which is your spiritual business here." There may be something to be said in favor of Professor Silliman's attitude toward interior decoration, just as there is something to be said in favor of a natural singing voice in preference to a half-trained one. Left utterly to itself the native taste of American craftsmen not infrequently achieved products of excellence, as colonial furniture, glass, silver, New England doorways, church spires, clocks, and clipper ships remain to testify. But the naïve expression of innate taste is no longer possible to us. We are committed to the conscious cultivation of the arts, and an educated sense of beauty has come to be regarded along with religion and science as part of the necessary furniture of the brain. An appropriate regard for externals, as in the lovely appointments of this room, cannot be entirely dissociated from our spiritual business here.

The old reproach that Americans were a people indifferent to art was perhaps never strictly true and is now thoroughly out of date. The concern for music, poetry, drama, and painting, established in this country during the nineteenth century, has progressively increased to the present time. Its scattered beginnings previous to the Civil War were confirmed and systematized in the closing decades of the century. One may distinguish stages in aesthetic progress in the United States: a stage of acquisition, a stage of appreciation, and a stage of participation. These separate phases, however, do not replace each other; rather the last two may be regarded as successive intensifications within the preceding stage. Each has left its imprint on educational procedure.

When Americans became conscious of artistic barrenness, their first impulse was to supply the lack by borrowing from the treasure house of Europe. In literature this stage is well represented by Longfellow's wholesale importations of poetic materials from the storied past of the Old World and of literary methods imitated from writers overseas. His efforts resulted in some odd blends, as when the Algonquin myths were combined with a verse-form native to Finland or the idyl of John Alden and Priscilla Mullins set to the measure of the *Odyssey*. The wealth created by the industrial expansion subsequent to the Civil War resulted in a sudden ostentatious architecture which dotted the American landscape with French châteaus and Roman baths. It also made possible the endowment of museums, art galleries, philharmonic societies, and the foreign-language opera; and notable private collections of paintings, sculpture, ceramics, textiles, *objets d'art*, and rare books came into existence. The movement of acquisition, which only now for the first time shows signs of flagging, has left us rich in relics of the art of other lands.

Few colleges were prosperous enough to compete with the great collectors, but the public interest in art products communicated itself to educational institutions and commonly led to the formation of college art galleries, however modest. Amherst, under the leadership of a professor of Greek, Richard Henry Mather, secured a well-chosen group of plaster casts illustrating some of the notable monuments of sculpture. The process of acquisition is still going on, most remarkably in recent years in the gathering of a representative series of modern paintings to which the late

Poetry and Civilization

George D. Pratt liberally contributed, though several important gaps remain to be filled. Moreover, some of the great private collections have been bequeathed to colleges, and in that respect Amherst has been signally fortunate in being made the administrator of the Folger Shakespeare Library in Washington, thus gaining a potential connection with a field of advanced scholarship in literature and drama. But one may note in passing that the possession of collections is not automatically educational. Imagination and constant energy are needful to connect increased facilities for education with the actual life of the institution.

The acquisition of libraries and art galleries and the opening of opportunities to hear music led naturally to a desire to understand and appreciate the arts. In this direction education was needed, and the colleges came rather slowly to recognition of their opportunity to perform a public service. In Amherst a chair of "Rhetoric, Oratory, and English Literature" was established in 1825, but the teaching of literature can hardly be said to have begun until Professor Heman Humphrey Neill placed it on a modern basis in the middle eighties. Previous to that time, however, the College had placed great stress on the art of oratory, and the success of its graduates in the pulpit and on the platform was a testimony to the excellence of their training. The pioneer instructor of music was appointed in 1894. An instructor of dramatics was not appointed until 1919, or an instructor of fine arts until 1930.

The adaptation of the arts to a college curriculum has raised problems in incommensurable values which one of my colleagues has aptly hit off by the query, "How are you going to make Keats hard?" In my opinion these problems will remain incapable of a thoroughly satisfactory solution

118

as long as faculties start with the assumption that the
proper discipline of the imagination through the arts is a
flabby thing and needs bolstering up by a heavy apparatus
of historical or analytical method. Keats can be made hard,
no doubt, if taken as a text for the study of English phi-
lology or as material for biographical or historical research,
but only if we are willing that his poetry as poetry should
suffer from academic desiccation. The teaching of literature very commonly falls a victim to the demand that it
conform to a traditional system of courses and credits with
the accompanying implication that the student earn his
credit by mastering at least sixty per cent of the information that his instructor hands out. I am outside my field
in speaking of the other arts, and so subject to correction,
but my impression is that college courses in music and the
fine arts frequently substitute for the discipline imposed
by the art itself an artificial discipline imposed from without. If that is true, they are no less exposed than courses
in literature to the reproach expressed by Henry Adams
in remarking, "Nothing in education is more surprising
than the amount of ignorance it accumulates in the form
of inert facts." If it is impossible to teach science properly
without the discipline of laboratory experience, it is even
more impossible to get very far in the teaching of an art
without provision for some artistic activity. For the essence
of an art lies in the practice of it.

This brings me to the third phase of my subject, the
relation of the colleges to participation in the arts. During
the last generation both vocational and avocational interest in the arts has greatly increased. Professional careers
have opened in unsuspected directions, as in landscape
gardening, commercial designing, interior decoration, and

fine printing, and many of these occupations appeal strongly to college-trained men. Without consulting our Address List I can easily call to mind Amherst graduates of the past twenty years who have become poets, novelists, playwrights, actors, play producers, singers, composers, painters, sculptors, architects, and curators of art museums or who have found professional careers in the useful arts or who have taught art in one or another of its branches. This situation is not peculiar to Amherst.

The demands of a college's clientele will sooner or later determine its policy. In education, perhaps more slowly than in some other occupations, we come at last to want to do what it has been evident for some time that we must do. Relatively conservative as Amherst has been, it has not hitherto failed to respond to new social demands, and in some instances it has notably taken the lead in responding to them. One may mention the erection of this building in 1848 as a response to the growing sense of importance of the physical sciences. At that time no one foresaw the development of a department of physical education, of athletic teams, or of intramural sports. Yet in less than a century Amherst has constructed three athletic fields, has built four buildings and is now contemplating a fifth for this purpose alone, and today carries on its faculty roll more instructors of physical education than of Latin and Greek combined. This last fact would doubtless have shocked President Hitchcock's faculty, but it has come about not in consequence of any sudden change of policy but by a simple and natural evolution. The pioneer work in physical education, initiated by President Stearns and ably executed by "Old Doc," is from our point of view one of the finest achievements in Amherst's tradition.

Arts in the Curriculum

A similar development in the field of the arts would have two results, one educational, the other social, which in conclusion I may briefly indicate. The discipline of participation in artistic activities, like the discipline of athletic sports, is one which appeals to students who have the necessary special aptitudes, in which skill is acquired by practice, and achievement tested impersonally by public performance. In the subjects of the curriculum we consider it so important that a student's mind should master the facts of science or language that we tolerate imperfect performance as the price that must be paid, humanly speaking, for enlisting his co-operation. But the world outside the college is impatient of imperfection. Is it not important therefore that plastic minds should become early aware of situations that by their very nature demand one-hundred-per-cent performance? It is not enough that an actor should know sixty-five per cent of his cues, nor can a musician get a B by striking eighty per cent of his notes right. In this respect the discipline of the athletic field and of the studio coincide, and both are an invaluable supplement to the educational experience provided by the traditional curriculum. Moreover, to successful achievement in sports or arts is attached a glory which is one of the strongest incentives to effort that a man can know. We cannot have too much of it around a college.

Nor can there be too much artistic interest and artistic activity in American society. One of the most painful changes that our generation has had to witness as we grow older and the world grows worse is the stiffening of intention on the part of nations and classes, until it looks as though modern society had no place for reasonable men but was shortly to become a battle ground of warring pressure groups. In a community of fixed and servile minds there can be little scope for education. It is no wonder, therefore, that President Conant of Harvard in a speech at Amherst in January 1935, warned the colleges to look to their defenses against the obscurantism that inevitably attends upon economic insecurity. In the same address he urged the colleges to promote debate in the fields of philosophy, social sciences, and the humanities, and quoted a letter written by William James recommending an open conflict of rival doctrines in the academic arena. But it is possible to overestimate the effectiveness of a clash of minds. The early nineteenth century held that the world was to be saved by powerful preaching, the later nineteenth century hoped that it might be saved by debate. But argument in general is an analytical process, more potent to destroy than to create living values. Justice Holmes was wise in his familiar contention that men live by symbols. It is the province of the arts to create symbols that insensibly work upon men's imaginations, and in that ministry to afford a means of preserving the persons engaged in artistic activity from the degradation of restless impotence. Not long ago we entertained a group of men and women from Michigan who sang a program of Elizabethan songs in honor of Shakespeare's birthday with obvious pleasure to themselves and with a perfection that delighted their audience. One teacher working for a quarter of a century at the Normal School at Ypsilanti has spread a love of music through the whole state of Michigan and raised the plain people to the dignity of distinguished performance. An influence of that sort radiating from this college would be the most perfect of memorials to a man in whom devotion to his Alma Mater and devotion to art were harmoniously combined.

The Future

of the American Novel[1]

THE subject assigned me on this occasion might appall a stouter heart than mine if it were interpreted as an invitation to foretell the future of novel-writing in this country. American novelists are not likely to take direction from anyone, and that is as it should be. Where a vital art is concerned, the steps in its progress are before the event unpredictable, and after the event inevitable—or seemingly so. A new achievement in literature comes always as a surprise, and one kind of criticism consists of explaining afterward that it was a surprise we had coming to us. So I am aware that I had better not ven-

[1] An address given at the Fourth Annual Writers' Conference held at Grinnell College in April 1949. The exact title as printed in the program was "What Direction Should the American Novelist Take?"

123

ture on prediction—not if I want to keep any honor as a prophet.

Still less would it avail me to lay down specifications for the type of novel which, in the opinion of an elderly professor, young writers ought to be producing. That sort of thing has sometimes been tried, but never, I think, with happy results. During the 1930's, for example, there were many efforts to define in advance the much desired Proletarian Novel. But by the time the blueprints had been discussed and amended and elaborated and tested by the party line and finally perfected, the hopeful project had attained the condition of a long dead fish. The few attempts to concoct a novel according to the prescribed pattern were too wooden for even devout Communists to swallow, and that is saying a good deal. The winds of fiction will blow as they list, and we must not suppose that we can deflect them by taking thought.

Yet in a modest and tentative way we may survey the field of prose fiction to see if we can determine where the ground has been exhausted and where it still promises to yield a repaying crop. I propose to examine the novel functionally, and to discuss three of its possibilities, which I shall call the aesthetic, the psychological, and the symbolic. But before we begin cutting timber there is a good bit of underbrush to be cleared away.

First, let us be quite clear about what we are considering. I am speaking only of novels which attain the status of genuine works of art. Perhaps nine-tenths or more of what is commercially classified as fiction does not belong in that category. I am, of course, ruling out murder mysteries, "Westerns," and all varieties of sentimental romance supplied for the delectation of people who indulge in reading as a form of daydreaming. I am also ruling out books of a higher type where the fictional form is merely a veneer applied to biography, history, sociological investigation, political propaganda, philosophy, or religion. Many of these works are timely, interesting, or important in their own right for what they have to say, but they are not important as true novels. I need hardly add that a genuine novel may contain a topical thesis as a subordinate element in its composition. Dickens or Steinbeck (at times) may serve to remind us of how skillfully such a fusion may be effected. But the pseudo-novel, of which a classic instance might be Bellamy's *Looking Backward*, is quite another thing, and for all its current prevalence it is not what I am interested in discussing.

If the line between a true novel of purpose and a manifesto disguised as fiction seems difficult to draw, let us say that the pragmatic test of a true novel is that it may be read a second or third or tenth time with increasing perception of new insights. This is the difference between journalism and literature, each of which may be good in its own way. The journalist communicates information, but the creative writer starts a chain reaction in the reader's mind which continuously and cumulatively expands the significance of what is said. Hence in a true work of literature—novel, play, or poem—the method of expression is inseparable from the content. The bare theme of a novel may be separately stated, but the effect of a novel can be conveyed only by the complete novel. It is in itself a unique experience for which no other experience can be substituted, any more than one can reproduce a symphony by whistling.

By metaphor and symbol, by appropriate diction and rhythm, by parallelisms and contrasts and many other technical devices, a novelist can fill the reader's mind with what David Daiches in his *A Study of Literature* has finely called "reverberating meanings," that is, meaning over and above the literal sense of the words. And the same critic goes on to describe the psychological impact of a piece of literature in such a discerning way that I quote him verbatim:

But the true creative writer drops his words into our mind like stones in a pool, and the ever-widening circles of meaning eventually ring round and encompass the store of our own experience. And—to continue the metaphor—in doing so they provide a new context for familiar things, and what has been lying half dead in our mind and imagination takes on new life in virtue of its new context, so that we not only recognize what we feel we knew but see the familiar take on rich and exciting new meanings.

The point just stated is fundamental. It touches the essence of creative communication, the method of the novelist. It is worth emphasizing by illustration.

Take something very familiar. You have all seen an ordinary, middle-aged woman who has spent her life on the farm or in a small country town. It is easy to picture her as bustling, competent, a bit battered by experience, if we think only of her superficial appearance. But to those who know her intimately there is another side of her nature which may perhaps be suggested by the word motherly. And in another context we know that behind the outward form exists an immortal spirit. It is the skill of the novelist to hold all these perceptions, and more, in mind at once and so to organize them that the reader will be startled by finding in the commonplace an unsuspected value.

Future of the American Novel

You will find it beautifully done by Sarah Orne Jewett in a chapter of her too often neglected masterpiece, *The Country of the Pointed Firs*, where the speaker is describing a Down East countrywoman, a practical and apparently not oversensitive gatherer of herbs, who in a moment of confidence reveals the heart's wound hidden behind her everyday composure. At the climax of revelation Miss Jewett writes:

She looked away from me, and presently rose and went on by herself. There was something lonely and solitary about her great determined shape. She might have been Antigone alone on the Theban plain. It is not often given in a noisy world to come to the places of great grief and silence. An absolute archaic grief possessed this countrywoman; she seemed like the renewal of some historic soul, with her sorrows and the remoteness of a daily life busied with rustic simplicities and the scents of primeval herbs.

Or in a different vein, consider a passage where the reverberating meanings are somewhat more complicated. Halfway through *Moby Dick*, Melville pictures a scene of savage grandeur. It is night, a freshly killed whale is moored alongside the ship, and the second mate Stubb, just returned from the chase, demands a whale steak before turning in. While he is eating it, he is disturbed by the splashing and wallowing of innumerable sharks around the carcass. Summoning the old darky cook, he commands him to go tell the sharks to help themselves civilly and be quiet—preach to them.

Sullenly taking the offered lantern, old Fleece limped across the deck to the bulwarks; and then, with one hand dropping his light low over the sea, so as to get a good view of his congregation, with the other hand he solemnly flourished his tongs, and leaning far over the side in a mumbling voice began addressing the sharks, while Stubb, softly crawling behind, overheard all that was said.

"Fellow-critters: I'se ordered here to say dat you must stop dat dam noise dare. You hear? Stop dat dam smackin' ob de lips! Massa Stubb say dat you can fill your dam bellies up to de hatchings, but by Gor! you must stop dat dam racket!"

"Cook," here interposed Stubb, accompanying the word with a sudden slap on the shoulder,—"Cook! why, damn your eyes, you mustn't swear that way when you're preaching. That's no way to convert sinners, Cook!"

"Who dat? Den preach to him yourself," sullenly turning to go.

"No, Cook; go on, go on."

"Well, den, Belubed fellow-critters:"—

"Right!" exclaimed Stubb, approvingly, "coax 'em to it: try that," and Fleece continued.

"Do you is all sharks, and by natur wery woracious, yet I zay to you, fellow-critters, dat dat woraciousness—'top dat dam slappin' ob de tail! How you tink to hear, 'spose you keep up such a dam slappin' and bitin' dare?"

"Cook," cried Stubb, collaring him, "I won't have that swearing. Talk to 'em gentlemanly."

Once more the sermon proceeded.

"Your woraciousness, fellow-critters, I don't blame ye so much for; dat is natur, and can't be helped; but to gobern dat wicked natur, dat is de pint. You is sharks, sartin; but if you gobern de shark in you, why den you be angel; for all angel is not'ing more dan de shark well goberned. Now, look here, bred'ren, just try wonst to be cibil, a helping yourselbs from dat whale. Don't be tearin' de blubber out your neighbour's mout, I say. Is not one shark dood right as toder to dat whale? And, by Gor, none on you has de right to dat whale; dat whale belong to some one else.

128

I know some o' you has berry brig mout, brigger dan oders; but then de brig mouts sometimes has de small bellies; so dat de brigness ob de mout is not to swaller wid, but to bite off de blubber for de small fry ob sharks, dat can't get into de scrouge to help demselves."

"Well done, old Fleece!" cried Stubb, "that's Christianity; go on."

"No use goin' on; de dam willains will keep a scrougin' and slappin' each oder, Massa Stubb; dey don't hear one word; no use a-preachin' to such dam g'uttons as you call 'em, till dare bellies is full, and dare bellies is bottomless; and when dey do get 'em full, dey won't hear you den; for den dey sink in de sea, go fast asleep on de coral, and can't hear not'ing at all, no more, for eber and eber."

"Upon my soul, I am about of the same opinion; so give the benediction, Fleece, and I'll away to my supper."

Upon this, Fleece, holding both hands over the fishy mob, raised his shrill voice, and cried—

"Cussed fellow-critters! Kick up de damndest row as ever you can; fill your dam bellies 'till dey bust—and den die."

Now if the grand intention of the novel is to picture the madly futile struggle of man against a cosmos epitomized as malignant power, you can see that this scene parallels in ironic burlesque the central tragic theme and so contributes to the working out of the whole design. But apart from its relation to the whole, the scene in itself sets up innumerable reverberations. We see it first perhaps as a sardonic comment on the humanist doctrine of the inner check. True, Melville did not have the advantage of knowing the works of the late Irving Babbitt, but just a year before *Moby Dick*, Tennyson in his universally popular *In Memoriam* had suggested that it was man's destiny to

Poetry and Civilization

> Move upward, working out the beast,
> And let the ape and tiger die.

But what if ape and tiger, like the sharks, refuse to die when bidden? Melville, you see, has anticipated some of the recent dissatisfaction with Tennyson's easy solutions. He has discarded Victorianism without waiting for James Joyce to give the *coup de grâce* by expanding the decorous game of lawn tennis into the portmanteau epithet "Lawn Tennyson."

Again, the sermon to the sharks inevitably recalls, and turns inside out, the famous sermon preached by St. Anthony of Padua to the fishes. As the legend is given in *The Little Flowers of St. Francis*, when the saint had spoken to them after the manner of a preacher,

anon there came towards the bank such a multitude of fishes, great and small, and middling, that never before in those seas, nor in that river, had so great a multitude been seen; and all held their heads out of the water in great peace and gentleness and perhaps order, and remained intent on the lips of St. Anthony.

We are told furthermore that when he had concluded his admonitions, "the fishes began to open their mouths and bow their heads" in token of reverence. This, of course, is all very charming, but to use a favorite critical term of the present day, oversimplified. Melville's parody indicates that the business of creating order in the natural world is more precarious than pious wish fulfillment would make out.

The primary power of the writer of novels who realizes his opportunities as an artist is to enliven the minds of his readers. This is both a basic and a thrilling function, and not less socially important than the work of the physician. Perhaps it is even more important that minds should be active than that bodies should be healthy. So in considering the present state of the novel, as I am now about to do, we are not giving our attention to a merely trivial matter.

First, then, let us view the novel as an aesthetic performance. During the late nineteenth and early twentieth centuries, and partly as a result of the prodigious efforts of Henry James, a master of the novel whose stature grows greater with every year that passes, the happy-go-lucky Victorian way of throwing together a fictional omnibus in three volumes and calling it a novel was replaced by an ideal of shapeliness. The importance of construction and of techniques of presentation, the novelist's bag of tools, were appreciated as never before. If it is no longer possible for even a third-rate scribbler to write in the offhand manner of, say, George Borrow or Anthony Trollope, we owe it to the painstaking labors of such devoted artists as James, and behind him, of course, Hawthorne and George Eliot, Turgenev and Flaubert, and several others.

But the English temperament, and our own so far as it is akin to the English, is not easily persuaded that entertainment should be mentally strenuous. We like physically strenuous sports, perhaps because most of us are in the bleachers looking on. But intellectual exertion as recreation has never appealed to us. Consequently we still put up with a slovenliness in some of our major writers of fiction which a less easygoing public would never tolerate. I like to think of the instant reply of the Irish poet AE (George Russell) when someone asked him what he thought of the poems of Thomas Hardy. He said, "In Ireland we do not think of poems at all until they begin to be beautiful." It would not be a bad idea if this criterion were applied to the novels of Theodore Dreiser and Sinclair Lewis, among others.

Until recently we have not been very sensitive to the immense possibilities of expression comprehended under the name of style. Indeed, we tend to think of style as only a superficial gloss indiscriminately applied which has little or no bearing on the quality of what is said. Actually a work achieves style when the writer's intentions penetrate down to and control even the smallest details of his writing such as choice of words, sentence rhythms, and tonal qualities. Style is the final warrant that the writer's mind was really possessed by his subject, not working mechanically or at random.

We owe an increased sense of the value of style to several influences working concurrently. One is the example of poets. Another is the insistence of modernist critics on the integrity of the imagination. And as far as the change can be laid to particular individuals I should say that the experiments of James Joyce, and to a lesser degree of Gertrude Stein, were responsible for a general awakening to the infinite range of expressiveness that stylistic modulation makes available. I do not believe that *Finnegans Wake* or *Lucy Church Amiably* are likely to be imitated *in extenso*, but either or both might easily achieve the status of Sterne's *Tristram Shandy* and become mines of suggestion to younger writers for a long time to come. And what they have to teach is that the great fascination of literature is its power to convey more than the literal meaning of words, a power which comes largely from the cultivation of stylistic skill.

A great advantage of the new emphasis on style is that

it reminds young writers that they do not need to rack their brains for an impressive subject in order to write an impressive novel. A quiet and simple subject is capable of extremely impressive treatment in the right hands. This lesson may be learned from Jane Austen and occasionally from novels produced by contemporary authors. I was struck by it anew last fall on reading a modest narrative entitled *We Fly Away* by a fellow townsman in Amherst, Robert Francis, who has previously written several volumes of poetry. The theme of his novel was the slightest possible, the experiences of a young man trying to preserve his independence while living as handyman in the household of a very positive, opinionated New England woman. Nothing more significant happens in the story than the young man's decision in the end to set up housekeeping for himself in an almost uninhabitable run-down shanty rather than endure another winter under the roof of his employer. But the characterizations, the atmosphere, the intonations of speech, and the contours of thought are so exactly rendered that the book remains more distinct in my remembrance than many more pretentious novels which I have read since.

If I were to choose one novelist of the generation just past on whose work coming writers might build, and especially in the formation of a sense of style, it would be Willa Cather. I would ask the young craftsman to notice how in each successive book the author works out anew the problem of form, letting her subject determine the appropriate tone and treatment. And I would point out how carefully every detail is studied, not with an eye to its own effectiveness merely, but much more with a view to its part in the whole composition. There is something to choose, I admit, between a slight lyrical novel like *Lucy Gayheart* and an epic panorama of the southwest such as *Death Comes for the Archbishop*. But no book that Willa Cather wrote failed to achieve a personality of its own, a distinction largely due to the beautiful flexibility of her style. As an artist in fiction she was not equaled by any writer of her time, nor can any novelist better convey a sense of the excitement inherent in great artistry. To her works therefore I would commend anyone who wishes to explore the novel as an aesthetic instrument of commanding power.

A second function of the novel is suggested by a quotation from the British author D. H. Lawrence, whose comment might be based on the type of fiction that he himself favored. He writes in *Lady Chatterley's Lover:*

It is the way our sympathy flows and recoils that really determines our lives. And here lies the importance of the novel, properly handled. It can inform and lead into new places the flow of our sympathetic consciousness, and it can lead our sympathy away in recoil from things gone dead. Therefore the novel, properly handled, can reveal the most secret places of life—for it is in the *passional* secret places of life, above all, that the tide of sensitive awareness needs to ebb and flow, cleansing and refreshing.

Viewed in this aspect, the novel becomes a kind of moral equivalent for psychotherapy. It is a way of letting air and daylight into the dark places of the human soul. It offers to relieve us of our obsessions by vicariously verbalizing them. Consequently it is tireless in its exploration of mental abnormalities, revels in the discovery of grotesque and odd characters, and finds its choicest opportunities in outbreaks of volcanic violence or in the narrowly averted menace of such outbreaks.

Future of the American Novel

The masters of this type of fiction in the United States are Sherwood Anderson and William Faulkner, both writers of considerable stature. Faulkner seems to me the more interesting of the two because his brooding over the dooms of individuals is accompanied by a lively sense of regional background and by a remarkable willingness to try bold experiments in fictional technique. Often his failures are as striking as his successes. High among the latter I would place *The Sound and the Fury*, a most extraordinary experiment in attaining enrichment of narrative by imposing four different points of view on the same sequence of events. But almost as important to the student of technique is *Absalom! Absalom!* in which the writer's method becomes so involved that it defeats itself. In general Faulkner seems to me most impressive in shorter units, such as *The Bear*, *Old Man*, and especially the robustly humorous *Spotted Horses*. I think it significant that I prefer to any single book of his writing the anthology that Malcolm Cowley has made from his writings for the Viking Portable Library. Still Faulkner, with all his unevenness, is a force to be reckoned with. It may be that he has opened the road that fiction is destined to travel for some time to come.

It may not amount to as new a direction as it seems. After all, the sanitative effects of tragic stories of violence and hideous crime were pretty well exploited in Greek drama. It remains to be seen whether the modern followers of Aeschylus can succeed as well in producing the Aristotelian catharsis which relieves the spectator or reader of his burden of pity and fear, or whether the extent of their service will be to provide a novel shock for jaded sensibilities after the fashion of the play based on Caldwell's *Tobacco Road*.

Lastly, I wish to consider with you the power of the novel to create symbols.

We are more keenly aware than the people of some preceding generations that men think mainly in terms of symbols. Our minds are not what Huxley fondly called them, "clear, cold logic engines"; rather they are pictorial, swayed by congeries of images and dynamic associations. Hence for some novelists the collection of the age-old symbols of folklore by scholars such as Sir James Frazer in *The Golden Bough* has supplied an inexhaustible store of suggestion and of usable material. The sardonic burlesque of the *Odyssey* in James Joyce's *Ulysses* is the most striking instance of modern fiction following the pattern of an old story.

T. S. Eliot has said that one of the functions of criticism is to provide our generation with "a usable past." I should say that one of the things that American novelists might be doing is to provide us with a usable present. By this I mean that they might select from the multiplicity of modern life patterns of conduct which deserve to be glorified and made attractive. It is proper that novelists should also point out the shortcomings of contemporary society, and no reader of Dreiser, Lewis, Anderson, Faulkner, Hemingway, Dos Passos, and Farrell can complain that they have neglected that side of their duty. But there is more in American life than injustice and frustration, and it would be a pity if our writers of fiction should become sensitive only to our failures and leave our real accomplishments to be chronicled by the daily press.

Just as Henry James made a career by searching through the international society of his day for traces of cultural sensibility, the moments when the flame of existence burned most intensely and purely, so it seems to me a modern novelist might undertake to find viable symbols for the strong energies that manifest themselves in science, medicine, technology, industrial organization, logistics, invention, and countless other directions. It is silly to suppose that the remarkable achievements of our age are the work of a race of blundering morons or baffled Hamlets. We may not know the answers to many questions that bothered Henry Adams, but somebody is enjoying the answers that we have. Something of that "life immense in passion, pulse, and power," as Whitman called it, should find a prominent place in our fiction. Carl Sandburg hinted at the climate most favorable to American literary art in decades to come when he wrote his tribute to Chicago, by no means claiming it as a heavenly city:

Come and show me another city with lifted head singing so
  proud to be alive and coarse and strong and cunning,

Flinging magnetic curses amid the toil of piling job on job, here
  is a tall bold slugger set vivid against the little soft cities. . . .

Laughing the stormy, husky, brawling laughter of Youth, half-
  naked, sweating, proud to be Hog Butcher, Tool Maker,
  Stacker of Wheat, Player with Railroads and Freight Handler
  to the Nation.

Where poets have led the way, novelists may follow. I do not wholeheartedly admire John Hersey's somewhat sugar-coated novel, *A Bell for Adano*, but it seems to me to have the virtue of laying emphasis on the elements in a total situation which deserve to be emphasized, namely, on the partial and tentative successes that keep us going in the midst of the inevitable waste and lapse of things in general. Major Joppolo seems to me to approach nearer the stature of a symbolic figure than the war-shocked Lieutenant Henry of Hemingway's A *Farewell to Arms.* On the other hand, I do wholeheartedly admire a novel of the present season which has quietly become a best-seller by dint of the gradual recognition of its intrinsic soundness. I am referring to Alan Paton's *Cry, the Beloved Country.* No one can say that the section of the world pictured in this book has any resemblance to Utopia. On the contrary, it is full of malad-justments, bitterness, misunderstanding, racial discrimination, and crime. Yet what emerges from the seemingly hopeless welter is the possibility of attaining, not any final solution of the social problem or any millennial state of being, but fragments of understanding and human kindness in a world largely given over to callousness if not to un-thinking cruelty. It could happen that the United States could receive an impulse to rebirth from the compulsive discernment of its writers of fiction.

So I would say what I can to stress the importance of improving the cultural discipline available to us in terms of artistic creation. The power of symbol-making must not be regarded as merely supplementary to other agencies of social amelioration. The business of literature is the exploration and perfecting of one of man's vital powers, and one which we neglect at our peril.

Though the analytic discipline of science and the synthetic discipline of religion, poetry, and art should harmoniously work together like right and left hands, for the last thousand years or so they have been almost constantly in opposition in one way or another. During the Middle Ages men tried to live almost exclusively by religious symbols, and the free intelligence could nowhere find scope for its peculiar ministry. Since the Renaissance scientific rationalism has been in the ascendant, and two major revulsions, the Romantic Movement and the present Totalitarian Revolution, have indicated that reason as the sole guide of human life is insufficient. Now the pendulum seems to be swinging back again. We are aware as never before that art must supply the symbols to sustain man's hope. Perhaps we have the choice of revitalizing and civilizing the imaginative powers or of having them break out of control in some new fantasy of world domination.

At the present moment scientific technology has created the most appalling destructive force ever let loose on our battered planet. To counterbalance atomic fission, the ultimate sign of nature's disharmony and convulsive force, may we not achieve also through art some potent symbol of man's resolute will to use division, as the cell divides, for life and growth, the process which nature in her better moments has employed to augment this world? Only the masters of symbolic suggestion can work that change.

For the year ahead—

"A stout heart and an open hand,
 Trust broadening out from land to land,
 Good care to keep our freedoms, and
    A modest hope of survival."

George Frisbie Whicher, *New Year's Day, 1948*

The Writings of

George Frisbie Whicher

Books

The Life and Romances of Mrs. Eliza Haywood. New York, 1915.

This Was a Poet. New York, 1938.

Alas, All's Vanity. New York, 1942.

Walden Revisited. Chicago, 1945.

Mornings at 8:50: Brief Evocations of the Past for a College Audience. Northampton, Mass., 1950.

Translations

On the Tibur Road. With George Meason Whicher. Princeton, N.J., 1911.

The Goliard Poets. New York, 1949.

Writings of George Whicher

Books Edited with Introductions

George Borrow, *Lavengro*. New York, 1927.

W. G. Hammond, *Remembrance of Amherst*. New York, 1946.

Henry D. Thoreau, *Walden and Selected Essays*. Chicago, 1947.

Selected Poems of Horace. New York, 1947.

Poetry of the New England Renaissance, 1790–1890. New York, 1950.

The Transcendentalist Revolt against Materialism. (Problems in American Civilization Series.) Boston, 1949.

William Jennings Bryan and the Campaign of 1896. (Problems in American Civilization Series.) Boston, 1953.

Contributions

The Cambridge History of American Literature. Ed. by William Peterfield Trent *et al*. New York, 1917–1921. Chapters on "Early Essayists" and "Minor Humorists."

Dictionary of American Biography. Ed. by Allen Johnson and Dumas Malone. New York, 1943. Seventeen articles.

A Literary History of the United States. Ed. by Robert E. Spiller *et al*. New York, 1948. Chapter 34: "Literature and Conflict."

The Literature of the American People. Ed. by Arthur Hobson Quinn. New York, 1951. Part IV: "The Twentieth Century."

Publius Virgilius Maro. *The Georgics*. Trans. into English Verse by John Dryden. [With an Introduction by George F. Whicher and Illustrations by Bruno Bramanti.] Verona, Italy, 1952. Republished New York, 1953.

Articles, poems, and reviews for various periodicals.